W9-DCC-139

Contents

We proudly dedicate this book to our mothers,

Mary Jane Parker and Patti Jo Fulmer,

and our daughters, Chelsea, Kelly, and Jamie.

We would especially like to honor Mary Durham,

who, at age ninety-eight, shares the wisdom of her years

while letting the girl within her shine.

Thanks

From the moment the idea for this book was born, we have felt a presence much greater than ourselves, guiding us, encouraging us, and blessing this project. In addition to the energy that power provided us, countless people have contributed to this book's unfolding.

To the thousands of girls and women from around the world who so freely shared their stories and themselves, thanks from the bottom of our hearts. Without you, this book would still be a great idea waiting to happen. Special recognition goes to all who attended the numerous writing groups and gatherings, where generations of girls and women were celebrated, and rich writings and creative ideas for the book were harvested. To our publisher, David Hinds, and our editor, Heather Garnos... many thanks for seeing our vision so early in the book's evolution. Your skills, support, and leadership are deeply appreciated, as are the efforts of the many other wonderful folks at Celestial Arts. Special thanks to Toni Tajima for the beautiful design.

Thanks to our friends here in Ithaca, whose love and support remained solid, even when the only words out of our mouths were related to the book! Warmest thanks are also offered to our friends on the West Coast, who are always there for us, pointing out possibilities rather than problems, and adding an element of fun to the journey. Dede Hatch and Amanda Brady, our photographers, deserve special recognition for seeing the vision of the book through the lens of a camera. Extra-special thanks to Hugh, Pam, and John, our legal eagles. And finally to our husbands and children...Dave, Russ, Jamie, Kelly, Chelsea, Noah, and Ryan. You patiently supported us as we altered our families' lives for over a year to devote time and energy to this amazing project. We are grateful to all of you.

From the Authors...

Years ago, when our daughters were first born, we looked into their eyes and recognized a part of ourselves. As females, we shared not only similar body parts but a woman's way of looking at the world. Mothering came naturally to us in those early years, and we were excited to watch our daughters grow from girls to women, just as we had.

Nearly two years ago, the rich reality of parenting teenage daughters hit home.

Adolescence is a complicated time. Kids start craving independence, parents have to learn to let go, and communication gets challenging. We began to question our instincts as moms.

Looking for support, we told each other about books we had read, workshops we had attended, and shared stories from our daughters' lives. We were trying hard to be the best moms we could be, but despite what we knew about child development and our training as family therapists, something was missing. The wisdom we looked for wasn't in self-help manuals on "how to survive adolescence." In fact, we were frustrated that many of the books on the market seemed to add to the negative light already shed on teenagers today. We weren't interested in simply surviving adolescence; we wanted to celebrate it. We wanted our daughters to grow up knowing themselves and appreciating their own gifts as women in the world.

After reaching for guidance nearly everywhere, we finally realized that the truth we needed was right in front of us all along...within our own stories and within the stories of the great women in our lives!

As a way to collect wisdom for our daughters, we began talking with women and girls. We invited them to write, to meet in small groups, and to share what it means to be a female in today's world. A tiny pebble dropped into the huge pool of women's wisdom created waves of possibility, and we became part of something much bigger than we had ever expected. Over and over girls and women said, "Thank you for asking me to tell my story." "I am glad to have the chance to pass on what I've learned." "Why haven't we done this before?" What began as a simple gathering of writings for our three daughters became an amazing treasury from girls and women all over the world. Intergenerational connection and collective wisdom became the themes of this book and its truth became clear: as girls and women, we are in this together.

A Message to Girls...

This is a book for every girl who is becoming a woman. Imagine yourself standing at a crossroads, in a place where many different paths come together. Behind you is your childhood: playgrounds, nightmares, lollipops, and secret forts made out of blankets. But standing here between girlhood and womanhood, your life is getting more complicated. You face new responsibilities and important choices. Hormones, peer pressure, and messages from the world in which you live can spin you around and make you dizzy. Just when it's time for you to take your first steps into womanhood, it's hard to know which way to go!

Becoming a woman is not always easy. There is no yellow brick road, no trail of bread crumbs, and no fairy godmother to point you in the right direction. But you are not alone. There are many girls and women who have traveled these roads before, and they have stories and ideas that can help you find your own way.

This is your book. This is your place to gather wisdom and to learn from the stories already written here. Let these pages overflow with the insights you collect, and you will create your own treasure map to discover the woman within you. At the end of each chapter is a place for you to write down your life stories and ask other women and girls to share theirs. Add your own photographs and art. Write down what you already know about being a girl. If you do, there will never be another book just like this one. There will never be another you.

You may not agree with all of what you read here, and that's okay. Figuring out what fits and doesn't fit for you is part of becoming a woman. Sift through these writings and hold on to the stories that stir something inside of you. This collection doesn't include every girl's and every woman's view on being female. Find out what's missing for you, and gather those stories from the people in your life. You can be your own teacher. Follow your questions and they will lead you down your own path.

There is no right way to use this book. You don't have to read it from cover to cover. We've included writings on everything from body image and mother-daughter relationships to sex and menstruation. There may be days when one chapter grabs your attention, and other times when you simply want to look at the photographs. There will be times when your life feels easy and smooth and you won't even want to look at this stuff. That's okay! It's a book to grow with.

We hope that these writings will inspire you to talk with girls and women in your life and to look for intergenerational connections that can support you as you grow.

A Woman Is...

The Many Faces of Womanhood

ow do you really feel about being a girl? For most of us, there are things we love about being female and things that we absolutely hate. For example, we may love that we are emotional beings, can give birth, and have deep and lasting friendships with other women. We may hate menstrual cramps, being seen as sex objects, or the fact that it's hard for girls and women to pee in the woods! Being female is a mixed bag, but we can learn to like it.

The girls and women in this chapter speak openly about the many sides of being female. Their femininity is celebrated, yet they also wrestle with tough issues like sex discrimination. They ponder difficult questions…when do we really cross over from girlhood to womanhood? In what ways are guys and girls similar or different? How do we honor ourselves as women and girls while still accepting boys and men for who they are?

Celebrate who you are becoming! Gather ideas from this chapter and from the women and girls in your life. Put them all together, and then take a long look at what it means to be a woman.

When girls get together, magic happens! The following poem came to life one morning when a gathering of girls decided that each one would say a word or phrase about womanhood. One word flowed into the next, and soon a poem was born. Let your creativity help you understand what it means to be a woman.

WOMAN

Flowing past peaceful water,

Wild wind, powerful and fertile.

Strength from the moon, mystical female,

Hips, breasts, belly, curved, straight, and kind.

Crazy, hot, cold, scantily clad.

Running courageously, active, yet lost within.

Comforting mother, beautiful woman,

Loving, healing, funny chick.

Sweet, complicated Me.

~*The girls of the Alternative Community School, Ithaca, NY*

Feminine

I appreciate what makes me unique as a woman. I realize the power in the softness of my body, the strength of my curves and valleys, my connection to the natural world. I sense the pulse of life in my blood.

I honor my ability to create, to bring forth life, and beauty, and art. To write stories, to make music, to dance, and to weave all the textures of my life into one. I learn to trust the wisdom of my emotions, washing through me like a river, cleansing me and guiding me down into the caverns of my life.

I see my connection to other women, ancient rhythms pulling us together. We bleed and bless and birth with each other, for each other, in each other. I am so grateful to be a part of this sacred circle of sisters. Soft and open, strong and full.

~ KATHRYN, 42

Let's Go, Girls!

Sometimes I think that growing up and being a girl are hard things to do. Even at my age, there are so many questions. What is it going to be like to get my period? How old should I be when I get a boyfriend? Do I have to be like my mom, or should I try to be different from her? And all of the friend stuff…whew! One day my friends will be in a great mood, and we'll be getting along just fine. Then the very next day, somebody gets mad at someone else because she played with you and not with her, and oh! I think it's all so silly sometimes!

There are a lot of things about being a girl that are fun, though. We can be goofy and play, or we can cry if we want to and nobody thinks it's weird. We can be really close friends, and be good to one another. We can be strong and play whatever sport we want to, even ice hockey and lacrosse. Girls and women have come a long way from how things used to be. Everyday, we need to say, "Let's go, girls!"

~ ALLISON, 10

Girls and women are beginning to celebrate themselves more and more. As time passes, opportunities that were once closed are opening up, and there is a positive spirit at work in our world. Here are some reasons why women and girls like being female....

"Women can reinvent themselves with the flick of a lipstick, by changing their hairstyles, or by wearing far-out clothes."

"We can do more things at the same time than guys can. They can focus better on one thing, but we can accomplish a lot more in less time."

"Girls can do both feminine and masculine things easier than boys can. The other day I was playing ice hockey, and got a penalty for roughing. A few hours later, I went to my school formal, dressed in velvet and lace and high heels. Could a boy do that? I doubt it!"

"If you cry during a movie, no one thinks it's weird."

"Women and girls can walk arm in arm, or even greet one another in public with a kiss, and no one thinks it's strange. I never see guys doing that."

"We feel powerful because of all the years that we weren't allowed to be ourselves. Anything is possible for girls and women now!"

Curves

There are many things I enjoy about being a woman. The curves of the female body are incredible… flowing lines, like ocean waves as they hit the rocks and the sand. The bodies of men seem to be filled with more angles and sharp edges. Women's bodies often flow from one part to another, gently curving away from their centers.

As a woman, I feel such a connection with the moon and its cycles. It controls my rhythms month by month, at the same time overseeing Mother Nature's tides. How incredible this is! My singular body and all of nature are one with the moon.

~ ANONYMOUS, 19

Celebrate!

I celebrate my life as a woman each and every day!

I'm glad the Earth holds a wide variety of people, especially female and male. But when it comes right down to it, I feel like I pulled the longest straw, rolled the highest dice, won the ultimate race in this life by being given the chance to be called "woman."

I am a risk-taker, I am strong. I feel, I dance, I express myself, without hesitation. I give birth, I comfort, I hold tight and try to know when to let go. I can be feather-soft or granite-hard, and both are equally acceptable. I balance demands from twelve different directions without crashing from the weight of it all. Being a woman brings challenges, too, but we all have the power within us to meet head-on whatever falls into our paths.

Womanhood is a wonderful place to spend a life!

~ ELLEN, 52, FEMINIST

Being Female Is a Plus!

There are many positives about being a female in our society today. I wouldn't consider myself a "poster child" for femininity. However, some aspects of my femaleness are extremely valuable. Women are often sensitive, emotional creatures who know how to understand each other. I like that my few close friends are in touch with what I am going through. Being female provides a basis for understanding moods, actions, and feelings. Being emotional doesn't mean we are weak. Women can be strong and confident, while being sensitive and intuitive.

I also like that as a female, I sometimes get to be taken care of. I like to be in charge, yet it feels good to have someone else take over once in a while. I like when my boyfriend opens the door for me, yet I also do it for him. I don't consider myself delicate, and I don't wait around for things to happen to me, yet the few times I have been asked out on an actual date and the man paid for everything, it made me glad to be a woman. It's fun when I can say, "So this is what it is like to be treated like a lady!"

My male friends say they like being male because they have the upper hand in society. They feel that they are respected more than women are sometimes. However, these friends also say that this is the part of being male that they like the least! They feel that men sometimes have too much responsibility on their shoulders, and also dislike being stereotyped as non-feeling, cold human beings. They feel they deserve to be considered emotional as well.

~ JODI, 19

Girls have many ideas about when they can officially be called "women." Are we no longer girls when we are eighteen and legally adults? Is it when we begin to menstruate, or when we first see our male friends in a different way? Certain events in our lives make this change more real to us, but the emotional journey is not so clear....

When?

Funny, it seems that no one can really say at what point a girl becomes a woman. Some say it's when she first gets her period. I remember sitting in a dark room, playing Truth or Dare with my cousins. The question was asked, "Are you a woman?" What they meant was, "Have you gotten your period yet?" To say it that way made us laugh, but in many ways, you are a woman when you have it. Others say you are a woman when you turn eighteen. When you can vote...or when you go away to college. But maybe it's when you turn Sweet Sixteen. You can learn to drive then...does that mean you are a woman?

Sometimes I feel as though I am trudging through life. It all goes so slowly. When will I be grown up? When will I be a woman?

~ CAITLYN, 14

Leaving My Cocoon

Something's changing deep inside of me, and I don't really know what it is, when it began, or how to describe it. I think I'm moving further away from my childhood, and it feels like I'm slowly, secretly losing something very familiar and safe. I'm sad, confused, and scared, but I'm also a little bit excited about who I'm becoming. I'm in my cocoon, and the next step is to change into a butterfly. For the first time, I'll be able to fly! But all I've known is life as a caterpillar, with lots of tiny legs to hold me to the ground.

I've always wondered how two creatures so different could even be related. One crawls along the ground or on leaves; the other is able to fly above the treetops. They sure don't seem to have much in common. The "me" that I'm used to and comfortable with and the "me" that I'm becoming seem pretty different, too. But as a young woman, I'll have wings! And hopefully I'll always remember these days before my wings appeared.

~ LATRISHA, 15

Keeping Her Inside of Me

I still feel like a girl sometimes, but I am thirty years old! You would think I'd know for sure that I am a woman now. I remember feeling like I was moving closer to womanhood when I was given many more responsibilities around the house. Moving away from home made me feel like I had grown up, too. When I started to see wisdom in the eyes of every woman I met, I realized that I was also a part of that wisdom. What a gift it is to be female! But I love to play and dance and be silly, and some people think of those qualities as "girlish" or immature.

I don't believe that we have to lose the girl inside of us in order to become a woman. The girl who has been there since the day we were born will always be there. The woman will show up when the time is right.

~ MAGGIE, 30

It is natural to compare ourselves to boys and men as we try to figure out what it means to be girls and women. Are the differences simply physical, or is sex-role stereotyping a part of the confusion, too? Our relationships with boys and our opinions about males can change, and sometimes it feels sad to leave behind those times when our gender didn't matter at all.

Just One of the Guys

I grew up with guys...playing sports, running around, and wrestling. We would stay out until dark, playing hide-and-seek, basketball, and hockey in our driveways. I stuck out like a sore thumb in my gym class, where I would aggressively fight to be the best player on the team. Most girls would sit around on the sidelines until it was absolutely necessary for them to join in. It never seemed strange to me, however, that I was the only girl just dying to get in there and play. I had a great time!

When I was twelve or thirteen, I realized what separated the girls from the boys. People began to make fun of me because I liked to go work out at the gym with Dad. I loved working hard athletically, but everyone laughed at me. For the first time I looked at myself and wondered if God had made some sort of a mistake. Was I supposed to have been a boy?

~ ANONYMOUS, 18

Trading Places

Most of the time, I'm glad that I'm a girl. It would be cool if I could try being a boy for just one day, though. I would probably sleep later in the morning, not worry about how my hair looked before school, and throw on the same T-shirt I'd worn the day before. If I forgot to brush my teeth because the bus was coming, it wouldn't be the end of the world. I wouldn't think about which earrings went with which shirt, and that little pimple on my chin wouldn't matter at all.

When I got to school, I could just hang out with my baseball cap turned backwards, talking about which teams will make it to the World Series, and who was going to the skateboard park after school. I don't think boys worry about friendships as much as girls do, either. To us, topics like who's mad at whom, and who said something to Megan that hurt her feelings, and why does Cherise like Andrew, fill our conversations at the lockers between classes. Boys just kind of hang out, and never seem to be too concerned about the same stuff that girls are.

I'm glad I was born a girl, but I think it would be great if we could just trade places for a day. Maybe we would discover that girls and boys aren't that different, after all!

~ TRINA, 13

LETTER TO BECCA

Becca,

It is your brother...warrior, builder, statesman...
who's seemed a branch grown from my tree, so
alike are we to one another. No struggle too big, no
feat too daring...for he and I hold the reins.
We try to fix the world; never mind if it makes us weary.

But as I watch you, all girlish hips and flirty ponytail,
something stirs in me, makes me turn
and look again at this foreign creature of my womb.
You have no use for stones you cannot move. You
pet the dog; stick close to home. Sing easily, or cry,
whichever suits you in the moment. And with

hands clammy from the day's play, you caress my
face, smoothing the lines gathered there. Becca,
what is it that you know that I have forgotten?

When we walk together, your arm proudly,
protectively slips around my waist. You celebrate
us as woman and woman-yet-to-be. But Becca, it is
you who is the full moon, and I, a waxing crescent of it.

~Rhonda, 38, writer, poet, mom

Some girls and women choose to live their lives in a traditionally feminine
way. Others feel more comfortable in a neutral place, or even in the
"tomboy" role. Luckily, it is okay to enjoy all possibilities today. What hurts is
when others try to mold you into someone you are not...a frilly, pink
canopy bed when you really want bunk beds...pushing you to become a
preschool teacher when you want to be an astronaut....

Just Me

As a senior in college, in a class on women's studies, I was asked to write
a paper on what it was like to be a woman. I wrote a paper explaining
what it was like to be just me. Since then I have had many female friends
who have been extremely jealous of me because my parents didn't insist
on turning me into a "good little girl," or preparing me to be simply
someone's wife.

Today when someone asks me what it is like to be a woman, I still
have trouble answering. I feel fortunate that I was not brought up with

rigid stereotypes. I was allowed to become me, and not just what others thought I should be.

~ MARLENE, 49

Say Yes to Competition!

Take a moment to compare the way girls and boys are brought up. Boys are given cars to race, models to build, tiny armies to command and plan strategies for. Boys are encouraged from the beginning to develop and practice a variety of important career skills…competition, construction, management, teamwork, and planning, to name a few. Girls are encouraged to spend their time dressing and undressing Barbies, feeding baby dolls, doing their hair, playing school and dress-up. Girls are taught to cooperate, entertain, give in, think about others first. These are all fine qualities, but in the real world, we all need skills that both boys and girls are taught.

It is never too late to take your life into your own hands, and invest your energies into more than your appearance or finding the right man. Develop your mind and skills; say *yes* to competition! Take courses in subjects that really grab you. Put some energy into your incredible self and find that dream career. You'll spend more of your time with that than with any dream man! And I bet you'll be a lot happier.

~ NATALIA, 27, SWISS ART STUDENT

Hiding from a Hairdo

When I was a girl in the early 1950s, no one seemed too concerned that I would rather be playing outdoors with the boys than entertaining myself with tea parties and paper dolls. My brother was eight years older than me, and didn't seem to mind having a "shadow" who would chase after fly balls for him, or run and get the basketball as it rolled away from the court.

Eventually my mother realized that she was raising a tomboy. I believe she was torn between encouraging me to be myself and molding me into a "proper female." When she was growing up, she preferred milking cows over doing dishes, but was given no choice. She had to do the dishes. But still, she felt that it was her duty to teach me to be a girl. She bought me frilly dresses instead of overalls.

I clearly remember one episode when my mother insisted that my hair be curled. I spent the entire day avoiding her! I hid in my closet, crawled behind the couch, and generally delayed receiving a permanent. After a few tears on my part, my father stepped in and told my mother that he thought I was fine just as I was, and that I shouldn't be forced to have a new hairdo if I didn't want one. This was the first time I recall being confirmed as an individual, regardless of traditional sex roles. Even though my mother thought I should at least *look* female, she never again stopped my boyish behaviors.

~ MARLENE, 49

Like a Boy

"Your parents raised you like a boy!" These were the words I heard from my college advisor when I told him that I wanted a career in outdoor recreation.

I have always loved being outdoors. I grew up in the mountains of West Virginia, and I'll never forget the excitement of the opening day of trout season. My father always took me with him on this annual event. I loved to wade in cold streams, cast my fishing line, and hope a fish would bite! It was on these fishing trips that I learned many lessons that have served me well over the years, like, "Just because you can see the bottom of the river doesn't mean that it isn't deep."

Going to Girl Scout camp every summer also influenced my interest in the outdoors. At camp, I really felt that I was accepted for just being myself. I always felt uncomfortable in the role expected of me as a girl in school. I could wear cut-off jeans at camp, get as dirty as I wanted to, and enjoy being outside with other girls who loved it as much as I did.

In my current work, I take students backpacking, canoeing, and winter camping. These groups are co-ed, and I find that I have to work hard to help the students avoid stereotyping camp chores. Women *and* men can build campfires...women *and* men can cook and clean up. The attitude expressed by my college advisor has changed in the past twenty-five years, but girls and women still face barriers to outdoor education. A friend and I have spent the past ten summers canoeing in Minnesota, and in all that time, we have seen just one other all-female group. I do not believe that my friend and I are the only women interested in going on such adventures. Some barriers are slow to break down.

My parents did not raise me like a boy. Instead, they shared with me a gift that will last throughout my lifetime. They encouraged me to enjoy my days based on my interests, rather than on a role expected of me because I happen to be female.

~ JUDITH, 48

Many girls and women have told us about unfair situations they have experienced in school. Being treated differently because they were girls, not being called on as much in class, lower expectations in math and science...the list goes on and on. Think about your own school experiences. Do you speak out when something seems unfair?

Too Young to Know

In my freshman year of college, I had a setback. I came down with the flu one semester, and went to summer school to catch up. I took three history courses, one of which was taught by a Swedish professor. I read everything he assigned, did all the class work, and was given Bs on all my papers. At the end of the summer the professor called me into his office and said, "You have done very good work, but you are a girl, and still too young to understand my course. I can only give you a D as your final grade."

I went to the head of the department right away and told him that it just wasn't fair. He told me that he couldn't change a professor's grades.

I got a D, for no good reason. I have since learned that back then, girls in Sweden weren't allowed to attend school beyond the sixth grade. They didn't think women were smart enough. Luckily that has all changed now, but until the 1930s, no girl in Sweden could be educated beyond age twelve. How fortunate I was to have been able to attend college at all!

~ MARY, 97,
EXCITED ABOUT THE FUTURE

Girls Are Dumb?

"Girls are dumb!" my ninth grade science teacher would say, several times each week, all through the school year. I was fourteen and new to the high school scene. Maybe this was just how teachers spoke to "new arrivals."

I never questioned why Mr. Browne would dare say something as outrageous as that. Usually I had been the one to question things, to speak for the rest of us, never afraid to say what was on my mind. But here I was in Earth Science class, getting better grades than any other boy or girl, loving the things I was learning, and the teacher had the nerve to tell me and my classmates that half of us were just plain dumb!

I passed it off as some silly part of the high school curriculum, and tried not to listen when he would say it. After all, Mr. Browne was highly respected in our small town. And how I loved Earth Science! To finally know more about the things I had been interested in my whole life... weather patterns, rocks, the stars. But I didn't dare speak out for fear that the teacher would use it against me in some way, even though my classmates wondered what was wrong with me. Why wasn't I questioning this like I had questioned every other issue since kindergarten?

Three years later, in twelfth grade, I signed up to take Physics. The only Physics teacher was...Mr. Browne! It was now the mid seventies, and the women's rights movement was well underway. Girls were finally beginning to have school sports teams, and we could finally wear pants to school instead of just skirts or dresses.

Mr. Browne wasted no time in pronouncing that girls were dumb. By now there were only a few girls taking science, which meant fewer girls to speak out about his ridiculous statements. At age seventeen, I *really* knew that he was wrong to say what he was saying. I also *really* knew that girls were not dumb, for of the top ten students, five of us were young women. But he continued to say this throughout the school year, and none of us spoke up about it. This time we remained silent because of those unwritten rules about dating. It was thought that boys didn't want to date smart girls, and if you did date a "brain," she should have no common sense. I rarely raised my hand in class when I most always knew the answers, and was afraid to do well on projects or tests. And all year long, Mr. Browne kept reminding us how dumb he thought girls were.

Did he do this to make us angry? To spur us on to achieve more? Or was he opposed to the gains women were making in the world, and trying to do his part to prevent at least a few of us from succeeding? His message was not clear.

What I do know is that in spite of my love for science, I didn't dare consider science for my college studies or career path. I was advised to pursue a traditional career for women... nursing, teaching, social work. I still love science, and have remained curious about the natural world. Whenever anyone asks what I wish I had done differently with my life, ignoring my passion for science always comes to mind.

You can do what you want to do... you can follow your passion as you think about your future. And if science is where your passion lies, please don't let go of it!

~ DEB, 39, SCIENTIST AT HEART

People around the world celebrate life transitions in a variety of ways. Many cultures truly honor these times, and have created beautiful rituals and traditions to be enjoyed during the passage across the life span.

When a Girl Is Born

Growing up in Liberia, I learned many important lessons from the women in my life. Women were not treated as equals with men in my village, but there was an understanding among us that helped girls and women learn from each other, endure oppression, and remind us of our importance in this world.

One of the most beautiful illustrations of the way women honored their feminine power was in the ceremony that took place whenever a girl was born. Women celebrated the birth of a daughter in a special way because they knew that their own story would be passed down through her. Everyone in the village knew that women were the caretakers, and if a woman gave birth to a daughter, she knew she would have someone to take care of her as she grew older.

After a woman gave birth to a daughter, she was led to a beautiful courtyard in a secluded part of the village. Naked, she would sit on a large boulder, with her newborn daughter in her arms. One by one, the women of the village would carry large buckets of warm water into the courtyard and gently bathe the mother and her daughter. The feeling of honor and love that was created in this ritual was something I will never forget. I am sad that my own daughter was not born in my village in Liberia, for I never had the opportunity to experience this blessing. Perhaps by sharing this story with you, I will feel that special love that is found in a community of women.

~ SARAH, 44, FROM LIBERIA

In addition to the particular culture we are born into, the era of history in which we live also determines how we are viewed as women. Your grandmothers, even your mother, experienced life as a female much differently than you will. This story takes us back thousands of years....

Our Female Ancestors

If I had known about prehistory when I was thirteen, I would have had more strength to resist all of the forces that were trying to change my true self. Fortunately, there are many ways to learn about prehistoric times. Art, pottery, cave paintings, temples, ritual objects, and graves all have much to say about life thousands of years ago. These artifacts tell us that their makers were peaceful people who saw the female as divine.

You may have heard the phrase, "History is written by the winners." You have probably already noticed that many people...gays, lesbians, people of color, women...have sometimes literally been left out of our textbooks. It is important to remember to ask questions. Stay curious, especially if things don't feel right to you, or if it seems like something is missing. Just because something is written in a book doesn't mean that it is always the complete story.

Women in prehistoric cultures were valued for their intuitive ways of knowing. This type of knowing is difficult to explain in words because it is deeper and older than language itself. You may have once known something with all of your heart, yet you didn't learn it from a book or another person. Trust your instincts. Make your own decisions. Listen for the voices of the female ancestors within you.

~ JODY, 30,
MODERN DAY AMAZON WARRIOR

Take a look at the girls and women in your life…those you know well, and those you wish you knew better. We are all so different, yet we share many of the same feelings and traits. This writer is beginning to understand these connections….

A Room Full

I have a vision of a room full of women. We all share special things about our womanhood that no man could ever possibly understand. There is a feeling of being peaceful and spiritual, powerful and strong, mothers and healers. Men might have similar feelings, but they are expressed in different ways. Women are different from one another too, yet we are still connected by our womanhood.

We are girls, we are sisters, we are women.

~ DORIE, 14

More Than One Way to Look in the Mirror

Body Image and Self-Esteem

s a teenager, you've probably noticed that everything is changing, including your body. Suddenly you look in the mirror or gaze down at your belly and breasts, and what you see may not be familiar. Your girlish figure begins to give way to the curves of womanhood. You grow hair in new places. Your breasts become rounder and more defined, with dark, firm nipples. The baby fat that softened your features through childhood melts away, while your hips and thighs become fuller and stronger. New hormones flowing through your body affect you both physically and emotionally. You simply look different and feel different.

At a time when your body seems to be playing tricks on you, it is challenging to sort out how you feel about all of the changes. Sometimes it helps to slow down and take a moment to notice what it really feels like to be in your body....

Take a Good Look

When I was 13, I was lucky enough to have a funky older aunt I loved to hang out with. She was the "black sheep" in our family, but was still a great inspiration to me. Since she wasn't my mother, I felt I could talk to her about almost anything, and I didn't have to worry about making her nervous or hurting her feelings. My aunt gave me the following advice which, at the time, I thought was a little strange. Now I realize it was one of the wisest and most empowering things any woman ever taught me.

Softly and gently she said, "You have been given an amazing body that is yours to take care of and respect. In order to begin to love your changing body, it's a good idea to really get to know it. Someday when you are all alone, take some time to really look at your body. Notice your hands and feet, your belly, your thighs. Without judgment, take a mirror and look at your face, your back, your buttocks. Be curious, not critical. Check out your genital area. It is a sacred part of your body, which deserves to be known as much as the rest of you. You may have feelings about what you see, and that's okay. Your feelings are a part of you, too. Knowing your body is a big step towards feeling good about who you are."

These words, shared with love and understanding, were a great foundation for me as I grew into womanhood. I didn't always feel good about my body, but thanks to a woman who took the time to share her wisdom, I learned to accept this body that I live in.

~ ANONYMOUS, 40

Take some time to relax and experience yourself just as you are....

Angel Belly

They had finally left her to her own peace and quiet. She slipped a tape into the tape player, and it lulled her with sweet Hawaiian tunes that swirled around the room. She fixed herself a pineapple milkshake and sank into the smooth, bubbly bubbles of the bathtub.

She let her tanned tummy float to the top of the water, peeking its little eye through the hole in the suds. It was a wonderful tummy, pleasantly plump, with peachfuzz down and a button set just so. Probably the best that there was. The belly of a goddess. An angel belly. Beautiful. She closed her eyes and sipped her milkshake. Mmm...sweet!

~ DEVON, 12

Much of what we learn about who we are in this world, we learn from the people around us. If we are lucky, we find others who accept us just as we are and help us adjust to the changes we are going through. But peer pressure, difficult family issues, and the limiting messages we receive through the media can make it hard to hold on to a positive self-image. Remember, we have choices about how we see ourselves.

MORE THAN ONE WAY TO LOOK IN THE MIRROR

When my eyes first meet an image of me,
I take in the backwards picture I see.
Am I fat or thin, or tired or pale,
Dark circles, or pimples, strong or too frail?

The critic within gets in her two cents,
Examines each feature, I've got no defense.
But then I step back, and remember myself,
I'm more than reflections of somebody else.

I soften my eyes and gaze deep within,
To the image I see in the mirror again.

Into the eyes of this girl that appears,

Her beautiful spirit a little more clear.

I reach beyond echoes of critical voices,

And remember, it's my life, and that I have choices.

How I see me is up to me now,

So I turn, and I sigh, and I take a new vow...

To look beyond pictures of high fashion girls,

See beauty in each woman's face in the world.

And the twinkle of soul that I see in their eyes

Is the same spark of woman that I recognize

When my eyes first meet an image of me,

And I see the incredible girl that I see.

~Anonymous, 17

Ooooh, Baby!

The moment you were born, wet and slippery to this world, you were pure, essential you... absolutely one of a kind, full of spirit and love. From that day on, everything you learned about who you are in this world you learned from other people. When you were born, you didn't know if you were a boy or a girl, fat or skinny, smart or dumb, pretty or plain. All of those things you learned from the people who nurtured you and took care of you when you were little.

Some of us were lucky enough to have loving adults around us who were good mirrors and helped us realize who we were as individuals. But some of us were not so lucky. We were taught that we had to play certain roles or fulfill expectations that didn't fit with who we were deep down inside. When this happens, we can get really confused. Sometimes, even thirty or forty years later, when someone asks, "Who are you?," we stand frozen, unable to answer.

If ever you find yourself in a place where you have lost your sense of who you really are, stop and remember. In a quiet moment, reach deeply into your imagination and remember the tiny baby that was you, untouched, pure essential *you*. She is still part of you and always will be.

~ HANNAH, 68, EYES OPEN

Many women and girls remember the exact moment when they realized that puberty had arrived. Something important was happening to their bodies.

Something Big

I can remember when I was younger and my appearance didn't matter that much to me. Life was fresh and innocent. Clothes, makeup, hair, and boys were not that important.

One day in junior high school, sixth grade in fact, I was in the bathroom between classes. While sitting in the bathroom stall, I overheard some eighth-grade girls talking about their hair and makeup.

I waited until they left and I knew that the bathroom was empty. I went out of the stall and looked in the mirror. I mean I *really* looked at myself in the full length mirror, not just the ones over the sink. I felt so strange, as if I was opening my eyes for the first time. I was actually a little bit shocked at what I saw. I had never noticed how broad my shoulders were, and I wasn't sure how to feel about it. I never realized that those bumps under my blouse were actually beginning to look like breasts. I grew up in a house with mostly brothers, and considered myself a "tomboy." Suddenly that "tomboy" disappeared before my eyes. There was a young woman reflected in the mirror.

I had a brush in my bag, and some lip gloss, and quickly used both. I felt transformed, but happy too. Something big was going to happen.

~ RUTH, 24,
EARLY CHILDHOOD EDUCATOR

Suddenly we may find that we are becoming more concerned about how we look. We begin to pay more attention to our self-image and our physical appearance....

Seventh-Grade Formal

At a recent family celebration, as I sat surrounded by my husband, two teenage daughters, and seven-year-old son, my mother boisterously announced that she had discovered some important papers that she would like to share with the family. Before I knew what was happening, everyone was laughing hysterically as the following list was passed around the table. Carefully treasured as the first tangible evidence of my budding vanity, this paper my mother had saved reminded me how very tender the self-image of preadolescent girls can be. Feeling a little exposed, I was also deeply grateful for this timely reminder of the thirteen-year-old inside of me.

~ SAGE, 13 AND 38, READY!

7th Grade Formal

Get Home 6:00
Eat Well 6:15
Bath 6:35
Put on Robe
Shave Legs } 6:40
Wash Face Very well
Rest 7:05
Wash Face Again
Put on alchohol
Put on Makeup - CAREFULLY not too much?
deoderant - ALOT
Put on dress, slip, Stockings
Brush Teeth
Use Mouthwash - Alot
Check hair

Put on Bow
Put on Choker
Final Look
Put on shoes, coat ¦ gloves

Go, AND HOPE IT ISN'T A FLOP!

HAVE FUN!
try at least to
DANCE!

All girls and women mature at different rates, both physically and emotionally. Through all the changes of adolescence, it is natural to look to others to help us see ourselves more clearly.

Puberty Talk

Starting in fourth grade, the concept of puberty gradually seeped into the collective consciousness of all of the girls I knew. It was introduced in school health classes and by books our mothers gave to us. I already knew the facts of life when my mother handed the book to me. "Here," she said. "If you have any questions, ask me." Sure, Mom. If I asked *anyone*, I'd ask my friends.

Recently, my little sister and her friends were sitting in a tight circle in our living room. "I'm in stage two," I heard one of them say. "I am too," said another. "My doctor says I am in stage three." She leaned forward to confide this, and then sat up straight and proud. The others all began talking eagerly, comparing the stages they had studied in their books.

Suddenly there was perfect silence as they became aware that I was listening in. Heads turned anxiously, as if they were begging me not to tell.

I had done this with my friends, too…long sessions standing naked in front of the mirror, trying to squint our bodies from stage two to stage three. Honoring this, I said, "I used to do the same thing," and left.

~ REBECCA, 16

Never Too Late

"Humph," I say, pouting while looking into my full-length mirror. My eyes stare disapprovingly at my girlish figure. Even my best friend has a reason to wear a bra, but of course, not me.

Oh, how I want to run through some archway into the land of womanhood! But not me. Not ever. I feel like the tortoise in the tortoise and

the hare fable, just plodding along slowly. But unlike that lucky turtle, I
don't have a chance of making it to the finish line first.

~ TREVOR, 12, FUNNY,
WANTS TO BE A DOCTOR

Scars and Flaws

The older I get, the more connections I have with other women, and the
more I appreciate my female friends. Gone is the awkward shyness of our
bodies. Now we wander through the locker room naked and chatting,
everyone's scars and flaws there to ignore. We talk about labor pains, fat,
breast cancer, and family break-ups. It is comforting to know that every
woman has her own story, her own problems which she has dealt with
and survived, none of which are that different from my own.

~ ERICA, 42

In our culture, we are often haunted by images of what appears to be physical perfection. Everywhere we look we see pictures of supermodels with
perfect bodies and gorgeous hair. Women's and teen magazines offer
advice on how to create the perfect outfit, find the perfect guy, and even
have a perfect date! What a setup! Not one of us can conform to those
images of perfection. We can be left feeling as though we aren't pretty
enough, thin enough, or simply enough just the way we are.

I Am Only Clay

My eyes are wide and bright and my heart is eager and willing and my
hands are ready and able and I am only clay and you are molding me and
shaping me and stories in teen magazines about how you are only pretty
if you're skinny are shaping me and the homeless man on the street cor-

ner is shaping me and what is written on the wall in the girls' bathroom is shaping me and maybe I'm just afraid that the wrong thing will get to me and maybe I just want to mold myself but there is no stone to hide under where I am, so I build armor around myself and maybe if I trust you I will let you in but I am confused today, oh, help me.

~ JESSICA, 14

Fat. It's a powerful word that carries a lot of weight for women in our culture. We have been taught that fat is disgusting, ugly, and a sign that we have no self-control. Every one of us has fat, and most of us have been preoccupied with getting rid of it at one time or another. Obsessive dieting and the increase in eating disorders among teenage girls and women are signs of how we can allow our weight to take control of our lives. It is helpful to think about your own feelings about your weight. What is your definition of physical beauty? What is a healthy weight for you? Where have those messages come from? It is up to you to decide what makes you feel healthy and good about yourself!

This woman remembers when her own large size became an embarrassment to her as a teenager.

The Locker Room

I hated the locker room. It wasn't so much the physical place, although the barred windows and ice cold floors did nothing to make me more comfortable.

The beginning of the year was the worst…when everyone had to own up to what size navy blue, snap-down-the-front, elastic-waist gym suit would fit them. Oh, how I envied the girls who would yell out effortlessly, "Mandy Smith, small" or "Sue Swarthout, medium." In my own struggling mind, I imagined shouting out, "Jo Weiss, medium," knowing that my extra-large body could never fit into a size medium gym suit. Maybe I could order a size medium and exchange it after class. I even pondered cutting the tag out of someone else's medium gym suit and sewing it into my own, so that if someone saw it lying around, they would think I was just like everyone else.

After all, that's what I wanted...to be like everyone else. I wanted soft round boobs instead of pointy ones. I wanted to weigh 95 pounds instead of 135. I wanted a flat stomach instead of that roll of fat that hung just below my belly button. I wanted my jeans to hang straight down from my butt instead of sticking to my thick thighs. And most of all, I wanted to be able to wear a size medium navy blue gym suit, just like everyone else.

Why we had to wear those things made no logical sense. But then, when I was thirteen, a lot of things didn't make sense. This locker room ritual felt like some plot to point out who didn't fit in...to the gym suits.

Jo, 37

Jo's mother wrote this letter after she read "The Locker Room." Sometimes in telling our stories, we can set someone else free!

Dear Jo,

I just finished reading your locker room story. I cried for you, and for me. I am so sorry and ashamed that while you were going through those embarrassing times, I didn't sense your anxiety and pain. When I was that age, I felt the same way. I weighed the same, and my boobs were pointy, too. I've never told you this because the memories were just too hard to face.

When I was in ninth grade, I hated wearing my gym suit. I despised it so much that at one point I pretended to have a pain in my side to get out of gym. Two days in a row it worked. But on the third day, my mother insisted on taking me to old Doc Mervine's office to get it checked out. After the exam, the doctor announced to my mother that my appendix was badly inflamed and needed to be removed immediately. I sat up on the exam table and shouted, "I lied about the pain. I only did it to get out of gym!"

The next morning, out came the old doc's knife—and a very diseased appendix, covered with cysts! Thank God my guardian angel wasn't one of those completely honest ones! When you and your brothers were kids, I always warned you that you shouldn't lie about being sick. Some old doc may just take you too seriously and lop off something that you want to keep!

I am so proud of you for not letting that fragile teenage self-image hold you back. You have become a confident, whole, and strong woman. Even though I wasn't a very good listener back then, thank you for letting me know this part of you now. Your story has set my own beautiful, pointy-boobed, full-bellied teenager free.

~ PATTI, 63, JUST THE RIGHT SIZE

The first step in challenging a negative body image is to really accept what we are feeling. This young woman allowed the self-critical noise in her head to lead her to a place where she could create a new image of physical beauty for herself.

The Sculpture

I hated my body. I particularly despised my stomach. I had heard all of the stories about anorexia and bulimia, but I knew I could never bring myself to that. So I continued to eat and eat, while trying to shove down my feelings of guilt. I thought like an anorexic, but never lost weight. I finally reached the point where I couldn't be alone with my thoughts. All I could think about was how fat my stomach was.

Earlier that year, I had gone to a local art museum with some friends. It didn't take me long to wander off, exploring the museum and its treasures. Eventually I found myself on the fifth floor looking at a figure of a woman carved in stone. Named *Diva*, she was well-endowed in every way…round and voluptuous. I found her very beautiful. Her image stayed with me all summer, calling me to return.

Whenever the self-critical chatter in my head became overwhelming, I would go to the museum to visit Diva. Eventually I took my sketch book and charcoal pencil with me. I sat quietly with her and slowly began to accept my own physical beauty. As I drew picture after picture of Diva, I began to realize that the images on the page looked a lot like what I saw when I looked in the mirror…and it was beautiful.

Although I still had a long way to go toward loving my own body, drawing those curves on the fifth floor of the art museum gave me a great jump-start to a happy self-image.

~ LYDIA, 15

Cellulite Blues

Her dimpled bottom,

so smooth and round

like fresh baked bread,

makes me smile.

Why is it that we spend our whole lives trying to get rid of the very fat we were born with? The same dimpled bottom and thighs that make relatives giggle with delight when we are babies lure teens and adults into obsessive dieting, fuel a multibillion dollar weight loss industry, and inspire countless inventions to "rid yourself of unsightly cellulite." Isn't it ironic?

The next time I get out of the shower and glance at the valleys and rolling hills of cellulite on my butt, I will smile. After all, it has been behind me for forty years. Maybe it's time I accept that it is part of me.

~ ANONYMOUS, 40, SMILING

Girls and women experience ridicule and emotional pain because of many physical differences. This woman reflects on feeling out of place because she is thin.

A SKINNY GIRL IN A DIRT YARD

I was a skinny girl in a dirt yard.
When I was young, people would see me and comment,
"You're so skinny!"
They'd see my bones and think I was underfed, sickly.
Well, maybe I was, but only a little.
They'd look at me and feel sorry for me.
Even my friends, who I'd look at and see their
Plump, rounded, healthy, happy bodies and faces, and
Wonder why I was so skinny.

When I was older, people would still comment,
"You're so skinny!"
They'd look at me and see my bones and think that I was born lucky
Not to have to exercise;
Think I was lucky that I could wear whatever fashion I chose.
They'd look at me and feel jealous of me.
Even my friends, who I'd look at and see their
Rounded limbs, womanly bodies, soft, welcoming figures, and
Wonder why I was so hard and skinny.

Now I am older and people still tell me,

"You're so skinny!"

But now I don't know what they see.

I don't know what they feel.

I don't know why it should matter anyway.

If people turn off the TV, close those magazines, and

open their eyes,

They'll see who people really are.

I wish they would see past "thin" or "fat" and

Find out that we are all neither.

~Genevieve, 30, single mother

A time comes when we are ready to make a statement to the world about who we are in the bodies that we live in. Through our clothing, body piercing, tattoos, acrylic nails, hair dye, and other ways in which we adorn ourselves as women and girls, we find ways of saying, "I am me!"

But nothing seems to say who we are more than our jeans....

The Right Fit

I went to the mall today with my daughter. She had to exchange a pair of jeans that we gave her for Hanukkah. They didn't fit, she thought they were ugly, and she can't believe that I thought she'd like them.

We went to four stores. She tried on fifteen pairs of jeans. It was actually pretty fun for a while; me throwing countless pairs of pants over the dressing room door, my daughter yelling for bigger or smaller sizes. It felt like a real "mother-daughter bonding experience."

After about forty-five minutes, my patience began to wear thin. I kept trying to talk her into this pair or that pair, and she kept saying, "Mom..." with that tone that only teenagers have. I couldn't believe that a pair of jeans could cause such a problem in her teenage life! Some jeans were too small. Some made her look fat. Some were the wrong name brand, and others were "just like so-and-so's."

While my daughter was trying on the thirteenth pair of jeans, I decided to take a walk around the department store. As I walked, I began to realize what I was supposed to be learning here....

My daughter knows what she wants. She knows how to say no to me. She knows what makes her feel good. She is patient enough to wait for just the right fit. Suddenly I was impressed, rather than disgusted!

I went back to meet her. There she was, standing confidently in the dressing room door, smiling that crooked smile of hers. A pair of jeans that looked like they were made for her hugged her round hips. I smiled and sighed, and quietly said thank you for an amazing young woman who knows herself a whole lot better than I did at her age.

~ ROCHELLE, 44

Hair. We use it to express our personalities. It even affects our moods. A "bad hair day" can mess up everything! We braid it, extend it, perm it, condition it, cut it, dye it, relax it, curl it, and shave it... all to make a statement about who we are.

"When I cut my hair, I felt like I didn't have anything to hide behind anymore. It felt like an important thing to do, like I was opening up to my independence."

~ SARAH, 15

Cutting Class, Cutting Hair

Our hair had always been long, at least midway down our backs. But it was the end of the school year, we were all sixteen, and the time had come to make a statement to the world.

Joanie had decided to embark on a career in haircutting, so she offered to test her skills on the three of us. While sitting around the lunch table, we cleverly planned our secret adventure. When the bell rang for the next class, we took a slight detour out the back door, skipping school for the first and only time in our lives.

Thirty minutes later, there we sat in Joanie's kitchen, as snip by snip we watched our hair fall to the linoleum floor. Leslie's hair was straight and blond, mine was brown and curly, while Karen's was red and wavy. Joanie worked diligently, giving each of us the same haircut, although the three of us still looked really different when it was over.

We felt so free that day! Free from the voices of our peers, which insisted that long hair was cool. Free from our parents' opinions, since they knew nothing of our haircutting plans. Free from the heavy influence of boyfriends, who all thought that long hair was most attractive. We were free, and we had finally made our statement to the world.

~ ANNE, 42

Today, young women pierce everything from belly buttons to tongues as a way to express their individuality. The following story is a traditional ear-piercing tale, but it reflects the rebellious spirit that we sometimes follow as teenagers to show the world who we are.

A Bold Step

When I was in junior high, I pierced my own ears. I took a large needle with some thick thread and plunged it through my earlobes. The thread held open the huge hole. In order to hide it from my family, I covered the thread with makeup, and wound the end of the thread around my glasses so it wouldn't show. It worked okay, until my ears got infected.

One day, my mother found me at the bathroom sink, earlobes huge and red. She guessed what I had done. I couldn't believe that she didn't disapprove! Instead, she calmly expressed her concern about sanitation. I had not even thought about that! I took the thread out, dabbed some alcohol on my earlobes, slipped in some earrings, and eventually the infection cleared up. This was my bold step towards femininity and individuality in my high school, and I was grateful that my mom understood.

~ ANONYMOUS, 47

In the last part of this chapter, you will find ideas and stories about things that women and girls do to feel good about themselves. You may want to take the time to collect more ideas from your friends and the other women in your life.

Free Throws

Participation in athletics has always given me a confidence in my body and its capabilities. It has allowed me to know my strengths, and to recognize and improve upon my weaknesses. I enjoy being strong, even powerful! I like the feeling that I get when I run harder, achieve more, really sweat, and hit more free throws. I've known from an early age that I could count on my body, feel connected to it, and be happy with the way I look.

~ FAYE, 41, MOM AND
FORMER PROFESSIONAL ATHLETE

The Joys of Skinny-Dipping

We all entered the world in our naturally beautiful state of nudity. Skinny-dipping is not only harmless and fun, but it returns us to our true selves in a single moment. Floating in water again, we feel the fresh feelings of openness and vulnerability while at the same time enjoying the sensations of being naked in the water.

We were born not worrying about our bodies, and yet, as we age, few of us escape the message that our bodies are somehow "not right." How ridiculous! Skinny-dipping allows us to believe that our bodies are completely right. How could they be anything else?

~ ANONYMOUS, 40

Smile for the Camera

I recently noticed that I looked pretty good in pictures taken about twenty years ago, and I couldn't imagine why I hadn't thought so back then. So now my trick is to imagine myself twenty years from now. I suddenly feel so young, and I want to have my picture taken so I can look at it later and think, "Hey, I looked pretty nice!" I want my picture taken so I'll have a record of myself… so I won't be invisible anymore. I am suddenly beginning to enjoy this process of living, and the amazing changes that happen whether we want them to or not. We bloom and we fade, and there's a lot in between. It's always the beginning of something, and always the end.

~ SUSAN, 53, "GOOD AT THINGS
I REALLY CAN'T DO"

Sort It Out

It is important to be yourself. Believe in yourself, and most of all, love yourself…especially your body. This is a messed-up culture we live in, and very mixed messages are sent to young girls. I had to teach myself to love my body. It is beautiful, and I am glad that it is the way it is. I wish all girls could think that, too.

Life is so confusing at this age. Your body and mind are often telling you two different things. It's your job to sort it out!

~ ANONYMOUS, 15

Ways to Feel Good About Yourself

The following is a collection of things that girls and women do to feel good about themselves. These are all suggestions from the women and girls whose voices you hear on the pages of this book. Feel free to add your own ideas, and to gather ideas from your friends and family.

"Make your room at home a creative reflection of you. Surround yourself with the colors, textures, and images that help you feel really good."

"Find an older woman whom you admire and spend time with her. Go for a walk together."

"Get outside. Walk in the woods, and you will find your place in the world again."

"Stand out in the rain and get soaked for no good reason."

"I like to look at my baby pictures. I can't believe that I was so tiny and beautiful."

"I love to crank up the music really loud, and dance around my house!"

"If you are really upset, find someone to cry with. Find someone who won't give you advice, but just lets you cry."

There's a Voice Inside This Body

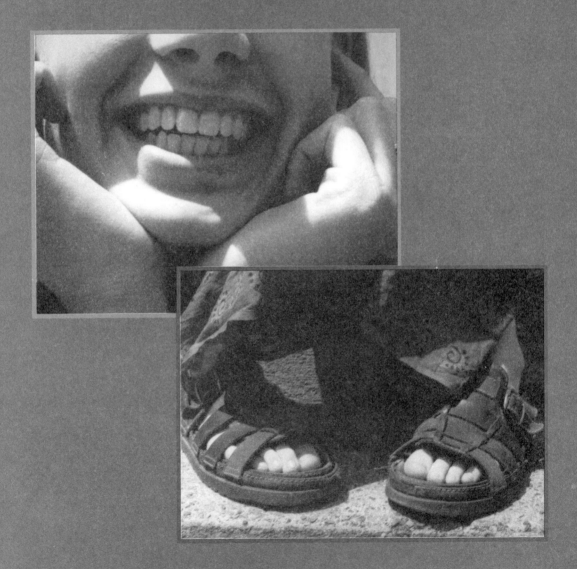

Holding On to Who You Really Are

When you were born, you cried out loud and clear, announcing your new life to the world. As infants, we express ourselves with total freedom. Many people say that we are closest to our true selves as human beings in the first two to three weeks of life. Maybe that's one of the reasons we find babies so lovable!

In the beginning of this chapter, you will hear women and girls describe how they experience their own inner voice. Some women actually hear a voice in their heads that they recognize as their own. For some, it is a sense of knowing or intuition. Still other girls and women identify their voices through their spirituality and their relationship with something bigger than themselves in this world.

When do you hear your own voice? Who in your life allows you to use your voice freely? Is it quietly hidden away, or do you hear it all the time? When do you feel most like yourself? Listen. There is a voice inside your body....

There is a voice inside this body.

I hear it all the time.

It's not just my conscience. It's me.

It's with me when I am happy and when I am sad.

Even when I can't hear it, it is there.

When people don't understand who I am,

The voice tells me they don't have to.

Only I do.

Sometimes I am mad at my voice.

Why can't it make people like me?

Why can't it make me be good at things?

But my voice says, "Be who you are. Be who you can be."

My voice can't stop me from getting hurt,

But it can help me speak up and defend myself.

My voice can be heard if I let it out.

I can talk, but sometimes I don't,

Because I keep my voice way deep down inside.

I don't want everyone to know all of me all of the time.

There is a voice inside this body.

Deep down inside.

~Caitlin, 14

What Everyone Said

My mother said, "You remind me of the sky, shining like a star."

My father said, "You remind me of your mother, as happy as
a clam."

My sister said, "You remind me of your brother, as annoying as
a bug."

My brother said, "You remind me of my friends, you always play
with me."

And I said, "I remind me of me."

~Kelly, 12

Women and girls sometimes hear their true voices most clearly when they
tune into their spirituality. This young woman found her own inner light
when she lost her uncle to cancer.

The Ball of Light

He was a monkey's uncle, or so he said. Now, after fifteen years of battling
cancer, this was it. He was about to die.

I loved him so much. We always seemed to have a deep connection.
His six-foot-three, bearded, bearlike physique always gave me a sense of
security and calmness.

He always said, "We are not human doings, but human beings." I
think he realized this after lying in countless hospital beds for what must
have seemed like an eternity.

Anyway, he was now five hundred miles away in a hospital bed, para-
lyzed from the chest down and about to die. I was horrified, alone in my

own bed, crying my eyes out. I needed guidance, and asked for the courage to see the truth of what was happening.

That night I had a vision. There was a great ball of light, the size of an orange, with a hand just like mine reaching towards it. Although the hand never touched the light, it was warmed by its glow. This light seemed to wash all over me and filled me with a deep comfort that released my fear.

I knew from that moment on that everything would be okay. I knew that the light would always be inside of me…all I had to do was accept it.

This light may take many forms for many people. However, my Uncle Kelly taught me that whatever it is, it is important to be still, to listen, and to "just be" so that we are able to realize its presence. It is in me. It is me.

~ LYDIA, 13

Through speaking out and learning from our experiences, we find our true selves. If we are lucky, we have people in our lives who listen and act like amplifiers to help us hear the power in our own voices. This young woman was fortunate to have such a mentor in her life....

"Question, Argue, Explore"

One of the biggest tests of adolescence is standing up for what you believe in, even when you feel like you are on the outside of things. Once when I was in sixth grade, my history teacher made a somewhat sexist comment. I raised my hand and said, "That is a really sexist thing to say!" My teacher was surprised, but ended up agreeing with me.

It was that same teacher who helped me realize that I had something a lot of kids didn't have. His motto was "Question, Argue, Explore," and that is just what I did. Popularity didn't matter as much anymore. I realized that I could speak up for myself.

~ CHRISTINE, 20,
JOURNALISM STUDENT

One of the strongest voices that we experience as human beings is what many women call intuition. Intuition is the ability to know something without any rational information. We just know. Hearing about other women's experiences can sometimes help us recognize our own intuitive voices...

"Intuition is like the electric current running in my house. It is always there. I just have to be still enough to plug into it."

"I feel intuition. It isn't a voice or something I hear. It is something I feel. This may sound strange, but I feel it in my left shoulder. It's a tingling feeling that won't go away until I pay close attention to something that's going on in my life."

"Sometimes intuition comes to me in my dreams. A dream can stir my imagination and I will begin to see my life differently."

"I have never felt a stronger sense of intuition than when I became a mother. From the primitive urges that I experienced in childbirth to simply knowing when the silence of my two-year-old meant trouble, I have been constantly amazed by how strong it can be."

"Intuition feels itchy like poison ivy. It bugs you until you scratch it."

Do you recognize any of these feelings or sensations? If you do, pay attention! They may be a great inner gift...your intuition!

Learning to listen to our inner voice means listening with our whole selves. Sometimes our bodies send us messages that our minds are too busy to figure out. Headaches, "nervous butterflies," sleeplessness, and stomachaches are just a few of the ways that our bodies try to speak to us. Listen to these symptoms before you label them as "bad" or something to get rid of right away. Your body, your mind, and your spirit are inseparable. Together, they are your wisest teachers.

The Stomachache

There will be times in your life when your stomach will feel like it's in knots. You will have what I call the infamous female stomachache. When this happens, stop and listen with your whole body.

Girls and women often assume that these knots are negative. We define them as nervousness, anxiety, depression, low self-esteem, and guilt. But before you apply these definitions to your stomachache, listen to your body very deeply and breathe! You may discover that the knots are the beginning of something positive, such as your spirit and soul trying to break free, your intelligence trying to find a way out, or a deep knowing that something is not right for you.

We are often discouraged from acknowledging what we know in our stomachs...in our guts! Redefine your stomachache. The next time someone tells you to trust your gut, do it! It is from trusting this place in your body that you will begin to learn about all that is beautiful in life and in being female. Your gut is the center of your universe!

~ GWEN, 41,
A CELEBRATOR OF WOMANNESS

I AM

I am not exactly who you think I am.

I am not quiet.

I am not shy.

I am not sweet and innocent.

I am loud. I am talkative and outgoing.

I am like the ocean, sometimes calm, sometimes wild.

I am a rose... watch out for the thorns!

I am a pumpkin, hard on the outside, soft on the inside.

I am a curious cat that loves attention but is also independent.

I am not the same person I was a year ago.

I am changing. I am different.

I am.

~anonymous, 14

Peer pressure, heavy family expectations, racial or sexual discrimination, and low self-esteem are some of the forces that can push our true selves out of our daily lives. On the following pages, women and girls tell stories of losing their voices, and share what they have learned about remembering who they really are.

I Lost Myself

I lost myself for three years of my adolescent life. When I was a freshman in high school, I met a popular, smart, good-looking guy who was a senior. From day one, I gave him my power. I was only 14 at the time. I gave him everything I had.

I remember a telephone conversation early in our relationship when he told me exactly who he wanted me to be. He wanted me to be his princess, his perfect image of a girlfriend. So, being the innocent young girl that I was, I became his. I thought that we were in love and that love meant "giving." Unfortunately, I had not yet learned that this giving should be an equal, balanced, give and take. I kept giving and he kept taking. I lost who I was.

Our three-year relationship was built on power struggles, guilt, and insecurities. He had a low sense of self-esteem and made himself feel better by controlling me. In turn, I lost all of my other friends, endured his emotional, verbal, and sexual abuse, and had no life outside of my relationship with him. I thought that we were in love, and since I was totally invested in that love and in him, it was difficult to see past it. While he was abusing me, I was losing me.

People tried to help, but the more they tried, the more I clung to him. My mother even forced me to go into therapy in the hope that I would realize what was happening to me. But no one else could convince me. No one but the one percent of myself that I had tucked away for safekeeping.

The "self" that I had hidden away could only take so much. I finally began to open my eyes and my mind to the situation. I began to see my boyfriend in a different light, and although I still loved him, I began to hate what he was doing. I realized that I was a good person. I was important, strong, beautiful, and an individual who had a lot to offer to the world and to myself...not just to him.

The one percent of myself that I had tucked away slowly multiplied, and I found myself again. I saw the light and grabbed it in order to keep myself out of the darkness. It took twice as long to heal, twice as long to rediscover my whole self as it did to give it away. Now, after six years, I write this story with my heart, soul, mind, energy, and strength, united in me...a powerful woman.

~ Amy, 22

A Hiding Soul

No matter how hard I tried, I just couldn't get it to stop. It kept saying, "Snap out of it. You gotta measure up. We don't have time for this. Remember, perfect is our goal. Be beautiful. Everyone likes a pretty girl. Think faster. What would they say if you were no longer an A student? Why is this so hard for you?"

This inner critic echoed through my head, and I screamed to make it go away. I looked into the mirror and saw someone I didn't recognize. She wasn't beautiful to my bloodshot eyes. She looked tired. Tired of being the girl whom everyone thinks has it all...a nice family, good friends, good grades. What more could anyone want? Myself, maybe.

So I started looking for myself. I pushed that critical voice to the back of my head and told it to go away. It wasn't welcome here anymore.

But it was still there. In the morning I found myself once again at the mirror putting on makeup (which I once considered a primitive mating ritual), trying to be the "pretty girl" my inner critic needed me to be.

I am still trying. I will always be trying to make the critic go away. Someday this maniac in my head will disappear and I will emerge. My soul, wherever I have put it, will come out of hiding and it will be beautiful.

~ Sarah, 15

I realize that sometimes I hide behind who everyone thinks I am. Now I want to be different from the way everyone sees me. It is hard to break through their expectations.

~ TAHEENIA, 17

If You Don't Have Anything Nice to Say, Don't Say Anything at All

My parents believed that this was a good message to instill in their five daughters. The only problem for me was that I sometimes had thoughts and feelings that were not positive and nice. So what was I to do with all of the other stuff that didn't fit in to the nice category? The anger? Sadness? Fear? The confusing part for me was trying to figure out what it meant for me to have these feelings. Did it mean that I wasn't nice?

As a growing young woman, I came to value relationships above all else, like good girls are supposed to do. I learned that being nice means saying only nice things. Nice is safe, it doesn't rock the boat, it isn't loud, or controversial, and it isn't likely to threaten anyone.

At the age of fourteen, I was getting really good at being nice. I had many friends, dated a lot, got along with my parents, and got good grades. However, there was a part of me that I had disowned and had forced to go underground. The anger, fear, confusion, the questions about sex, death, and the big issues of life were not up for discussion. They were messy and might make somebody feel uncomfortable. The little voice that raised all of these issues stayed quiet for many years.

It wasn't until I left home and went to college and heard the voices of others that I remembered my own. I finally heard a message of permission and encouragement to share and explore all of the parts of myself.

With a loving woman therapist as my guide, I learned how to give a voice to my anger, my tears, fears and conflicts. It was a painful, messy, complicated process, which was definitely not "nice." But I emerged a stronger, more complete woman, able to express and explore a whole range of feelings.

Twenty years after venturing into the darker parts of myself, I am still a nice woman. However, now I am able to say what I want to in a way that is respectful to myself and others.

I think the biggest challenge in becoming a woman is finding your own internal voice, learning to turn up the volume so you can listen clearly to what it is saying, and then having the courage to express yourself fully and without apology.

My own daughter is seven now. I will not give her the message that my parents gave me. My message to her is: "When you are still and quiet, you can hear your own voice inside really clearly. Listen carefully and it will guide you to speak your own truth." My hope is that her journey to womanhood will be a little easier than mine was.

~ MARY, 42, MOTHER OF TWO,
PSYCHOTHERAPIST

This young woman writes about how we sometimes hide behind masks that we wear in order to please others, afraid to show the world our true feelings.

TEARDROPS FALLING FROM BEHIND IRON MASKS

I sometimes wonder who decides

when it is time to cry.

We've all been taught to wear our masks.

Never letting them fall away from our faces.

Never letting the light of day

Slip behind the iron masks.

Never exposing our pain.

The iron mask may protect us from the storm.

But what happens when the

Random raindrops slip inside and

Turn our emotions, which

We have strived hard to master,

Into

Nothing

More

Than rust?

Maybe someday when all is safe,

Our masks will fall away from our faces

And crumble to the ground in a

Cloud of dust.

The tears will be allowed to fall

Freely.

Exposing who we really are.

~Maya, 17

There are many ways to lose your voice, but just as many ways to begin to reclaim it. One way that you can express your own true voice is by writing in a journal or a diary. Taking time to just write...about your life, your dreams, your fears and hopes, gives your inner voice a place to hang out. A journal can be a good friend. It never disagrees with you, and if you keep it in a safe place, it never betrays your secrets. Here are some stories about how women and girls have found writing in a journal to be a great outlet....

My Place

There were so many times when I thought I was the only one on the planet. I thought I was completely misunderstood and unloved by everyone. I was a master at wallowing in my sorrow, and made an art out of moodiness. I needed an outlet for all of my feelings, a way to express the turbulence that was going on inside me. I began to write in a journal. This was my place. No one but me could enter it. A place where I could safely go and not worry about whether I was wearing the right clothes, if my boobs were ever going to grow, or if I was friends with the right people. In my journal I could say whatever I wanted to say, no matter how mean, stupid, sentimental, cheesy, or sad...no rules. It was, and still is, my refuge...a place where I can just *be*.

~ JENNIFER, 22, CRISIS QUEEN

My Box of Journals

When I was a teenager, I had a very small voice. It was the last thing I worried about. The size of my nose, my behind, and my breasts were much more important to me.

My voice was small, but inside I had a great desire to express myself, so I began to write. The idea came from my friend, Erna. She was, and still is, a prolific writer, and one of my best teachers. I wrote journals, sometimes filling one up in just a week. I wrote in pencil, ballpoint, fountain pen, in Batman notebooks, and in serious hardcover blank books. I just had to write.

My journals became a collection of my teenage life. All of the things that I couldn't say to another human, I said to my books. My first period, feelings of alienation, crazy family, crushes and broken hearts, best friends, fears, and general confusion are all recorded in scribbled, elaborate detail.

After a few years, I learned to speak. Not loud, not well, and always with the fear of saying the wrong thing or hurting someone. With the power of speech gained, my once busy pen sat unused. Why write when you can talk?

All of my journals, saved for something, went into a large cardboard box, sealed up with packing tape and neatly labeled. More journals came afterward, but not as often. Then the stream of writing finally stopped, except for a few tiny spits and starts.

I am now 32 years old, and have begun to call myself a writer. I don't write journals, fiction, poetry, or anything like that. I write as part of my profession. But I still have my box of journals. I have carried them with me faithfully, out of my parents' home years ago, across the United States from East Coast to West, through many cities, to where I now live. In all those years and all those cities, I never had the courage to open up the box. The tape is intact, and I am afraid to disturb it. I didn't plan to ignore my journals. I didn't plan to stop writing them, either.

Why haven't I opened the box? It has to do with fear. Fear of meeting my teenage self again without wanting to escape in one way or another. I am afraid to see who I was, to see what I have lost, what I dreamed I might be and have not yet become. I am afraid to be disappointed. Still, I have carried the box with me, like a small cage of memories, just in case. Now it sits, waiting for me, and I think I am getting ready to open it up. One night soon, when I am all alone, I will tear off the old gray tape and visit that teenager with my face, my nose, my name, and see how she's doing after all this time.

~ MARIA, 32

In addition to writing in a journal, finding other ways to express yourself creatively can help you discover and hold onto your inner voice. Music, art, drama, and dance are just some of the ways to express yourself. Find what works for you and do it!

Square Peg

I was a skinny, awkward adolescent, weighing 100 pounds soaking wet. I was full of turmoil and emotions; I was a square peg in the round world.

I coped by writing poetry, often expressing my desire for acceptance and recognition of my inner self. I played music for hours, convinced that the lyrics of James Taylor, Gordon Lightfoot, and Cat Stevens were written in the same type of confusion that I held in mind.

In my junior year in high school, at my third school in three years, I took a risk and joined the Drama Club. At first I stayed backstage, building sets and helping with costumes. With the guidance and support of a caring teacher, I tried out for a play and got the part. From the moment I stepped on the stage, the emotional clouds I was experiencing began to fade. I felt that I was unique and worthy of acceptance. I was truly *me*.

Now in my thirty-eighth year, as a mother of two, a professional and wife, I have found my way back to the stage in a community theater. To my delight, it still holds its magic, and I am lifted by my uniqueness while performing. You can find some magic in the world for yourself, and when you do, hold onto it! Let it help you express who you really are!

~ SHERYL, 38, SOCIAL WORKER,
MOTHER, WIFE

Drawing Me Out

When I was a teenager, the act of drawing took my mind away from my problems. Every Sunday I would isolate myself in the dining room and spend the afternoon drawing. I was the only one in my family interested in art. I felt special because I had *my* paper and *my* pencils. It meant a lot to me because I had many siblings, and there wasn't much that was just *mine*. I felt proud and honored when one of my parents or siblings commented positively on my work. However, they criticized my art much more than they praised it. It was typical of them. They always had very high expectations of me, and I felt that I was never good enough. In my case, it worked to my advantage. It made me become even more determined and work even harder.

I still enjoy creating. Art helps me express what I am feeling and who I am.

~ NADINE, 39, MOTHER OF THREE

My Friend, Bear

I had a lot of good times when I was a teenager. What I remember most, though, aren't the crazy, fun times hanging out with friends. My favorite memories are of the hours spent out in the woods behind our house with my dog, Bear. I still have him. He is fourteen now, gray-faced and delightful. Bear and I have spent many afternoons walking, sitting, and daydreaming in the woods. Those times helped me find peace and safety in a world that seemed chaotic. Those afternoons taught me patience, faith, and love for the natural world. They shaped me into the woman that I am now.

I still make time to be alone. I call it my "down time." Without this time for myself, I feel scattered, tense, and tired. The woods are my favorite place to retreat. There I feel most in touch with myself…clear and joyful. The colors and scents are calming and help me focus on what is most important. There is no one to distract me, no one to please, to be smart or pretty for. I come back home feeling centered and full of energy.

Making time to be alone is not always easy. You have to make it a priority. A good way to start is to notice when you feel anxious or confused. Ask yourself if it would help to be alone. If the answer is yes, you might take a short walk or find another way to give yourself some space. Making time alone is all about your health and happiness!

~ MARIA, 32

Oatmeal in My Brain

Sometimes I love to be alone. I can't explain the feelings that I have then. I can clear away the "oatmeal" that surrounds my brain and protects it from the outside world. I can breathe. I can think about random things. I can untangle the knotted thoughts I have about the world and the people in my life.

~ ANONYMOUS, 14

We all have different places and times in our lives when we feel the most comfortable and at ease. In those moments, our true voices are often closest to the surface. Here are some examples of situations where women and girls feel free to be who they really are:

"When I am home alone, writing." age 11

"When I cry." age 17

"When I'm sitting in my rocking chair." age 12

"When I am working on my photo albums." age 25

"When I am out in the deep woods, walking and listening." age 75

""When I am spending time with my mom." age 16

"When I am exercising." age 41

"When I am at home with my family." age 53

"When I have just done the impossible." age 17

"When I am writing music." age 39

"When I am hanging out at home with my friends." age 10

"When I am naked." age 40

"When I am praying." age 88

"When I am performing and I am in tune with the audience." age 28

"When something delicious is baking in the oven." age 36

"When I am working in my garden in the spring." age 26

When do you feel safe and comfortable in your life?

The Birth of Knowing

True story…no kidding. It happened one morning as I started out for a run. I had taken along my bright yellow Sony Walkman so I could get lost in the music rather than in the pain of my first long run in a week. As I nudged the earphones into my ears, I realized that the batteries had died. The Walkman was no good to me now, and with little time or energy to run back up the hill to the house, I tucked it into my mailbox at the end of the driveway.

Beautiful day. Great run. Five miles and forty-five minutes later, I found myself back at the mailbox, reaching in to retrieve the Walkman from its hiding place. As I pulled it out, I noticed something very strange. There in my hand was a bright yellow portable tape-player, but it was dirty, broken, not a Sony, and not mine. I was stunned.

"This is like something out of the Twilight Zone," I thought to myself.

Perplexed and confused, I walked up the hill and began to figure out what had happened. Someone had been watching me, and had seen me put my Sony Walkman into the mailbox at the start of my run. Holding their own broken "wannabe" yellow tape player in their hands, the temptation of my brand new Sony resting in the mailbox undid them. Some time over the next forty-five minutes, two realities traded places.

Back in my kitchen, as I gazed at the dirty, portable tape player on my counter, the anger wafted in. I felt invaded. Taken advantage of. Someone had been watching me. Someone had deliberately stolen my Walkman in broad daylight. It felt real now. No Twilight Zone.

A couple of hours later, having walked by the replacement tape player for the fifth time, the disgust finally got to me. I swooped the filthy thing off of my counter and stuffed it into the garbage. I wanted no reminders of this event.

I had completed my letting-go ritual. It was done, or so I thought. Moments later, I went to the kitchen to get a drink and looked out my window. A teenage girl was opening my mailbox! Without thinking, I ran to the garbage, grabbed the "wannabe," and ran down the hill towards the girl.

"Hey you!," I yelled to her across the busy street.

She stood there stunned, like a deer transfixed in the headlights of an oncoming car. In a split second, before I realized what was happening, she started running towards me. When she came within about ten feet, she reached into her backpack and pulled out my Sony Walkman.

"I couldn't do it," she said simply.

I held out her tape player, and we traded places once more. "You did the right thing," I responded.

And with no other words spoken, she turned and walked away. As I walked up the driveway, the immensity of this event hit me, and I turned to watch her leave, wanting to hold onto this lesson. She too had stopped to look back at me. She waved, and I gave her a thumbs up. All was forgiven. All was understood.

As I look back at this true story, I feel blessed to have been part of a rich moment in this young girl's life. She heard her inner voice, and despite the weight of her previous actions, she allowed it to lead her towards her own truth. Honesty is the place where our true voice thrives. When we are willing to be honest with ourselves and with others, even when it hurts, we learn and grow from our experiences.

I will never know what possessed her to take my Walkman in the first place, or what exactly inspired her to return it. I would like to think that she experienced her own "knowing" and responded. If that is true, the moral decisions she faces from this day forward may be a little easier if she continues to listen to her own guiding voice.

We all make mistakes, but it is never too late to say you are sorry.

~ BUNNY, 39, THANKFUL

What I've Learned

My teenage years aren't over yet, but I have already learned some important things. This is a time of discovery, frustration, and questions. It is a time to develop my mind, body and spirit; a time to search for answers about who I am and what I was put on this earth to do. It's a time to find my voice. Here are a few more things I have learned:

No one is perfect.

Take risks.

Challenge yourself.

Be brave.

Don't be ashamed to be who you really are.

Be open and ready to learn.

If you are bored, ask yourself if you're the one who's boring.

Realize that you are going to go crazy sometimes.

Be someone you are proud of.

Learn from your mistakes.

Have fun!

Life as a teenager can be just plain weird. Sometimes you love it, but other times it is sad and nothing seems fair. We all get different shares of each. Remember to try to be positive at least once in awhile. No matter what, you are never truly alone. There is someone who feels just like you out there. Your life is a gift. It is yours alone. Dare to make a difference!

~ CLARA, 15

Fitting In

Peers, Friends, and the Social Scene

 riendships may be more important to you now than anything else in your world. A true friend helps you to see who you really are, at a time when you may not be so sure any more.

Your feelings about how you fit in with friends and peers spill over into every area of your life. Some girls feel as though they are being pulled in many different directions at once. They're absolutely sure how they feel about something one minute, then just as quickly, something happens and they need to conform to the popular opinion instead. At a time when we are moving away from the strong influence of family, we learn many valuable lessons from our friendships.

Friendships are great…friendships are complicated. What does friendship mean to you?

She Really Understands

I have many acquaintances, but only a handful of people I can truly call my friends. A friend is someone to whom I can tell my deepest, silliest, but real fears, without worrying that she will laugh at me or tell others that I am a jerk. Most acquaintances will help out when there is an emergency, but a true friend will be there when you just need to say your thoughts out loud. Male friends can listen when you're troubled, and are often very good at trying to find a solution to a problem, but my women friends truly understand my hurts, fears, and worries.

~ ANONYMOUS, 21

Girlfriends

There is something quite unique about friendships between women. We share a bond like sisters...maybe it really is a sisterhood! We have all had similar experiences being women on this planet together, and those experiences mean a lot. Women are also able to show affection to one another more easily, whether it's a hug or a simple clutch of the arm. There is a certain beauty and strength that women give to each other, which makes friendships between women all the more wonderful.

~ DANIELA, 19

Think about the qualities you look for in a true friend as you read how girls and women define the friendships in their lives....

A friend is someone you trust, and she trusts you, too. She will never tell your secrets, but in return, you must never tell hers. To *have* a good friend, you have to *be* a good friend.

~ ARIEL, 12, A GOOD FRIEND

Friends are wonderful to have and share a laugh with, but close friends are something to hold onto. They are precious gems. And although they may be "high maintenance" and need frequent polishing, in the end, they will be there to shine and make you feel great.

~ ANN, 20

The best definition of friendship that I can think of is from the philosopher Aristotle. "What is a friend? It is a single soul dwelling in two bodies."

~ MARTHA, COLLEGE STUDENT

Dolls, Donuts, and Boyfriends

One of the very first things a child learns about friendship is that you have to deal with kids your own age a little differently than you deal with your parents. Kids have a way of fighting back and saying hurtful things sometimes. Most parents try not to do that.

For girls, as you get older, you are no longer fighting over who has the bigger doll or who gets the best donut. You fight over boyfriends and parts in school plays and who got a better grade on the math test. Suddenly your life is filled with competition, jealousy, and mistrust. This can feel really awful, especially when your body is going through all sorts of crazy changes and your hormones are really racing!

So what makes a good friend? She is someone you can trust and communicate with, someone who is honest and cares about your feelings. A true friend can make you feel better, no matter what the situation. She likes you for who you are, and doesn't put on a front. A true friend is a person you can laugh with and cry with. She will always be there for you.

~ ELIZABETH, 17

Imagine yourself eighty years from now, calling a friend on the phone whom you have known your entire life! Sometimes we make that type of connection with a friend, and share many moments of our lives with them.

Lifelong Friends

When I was a young girl, I had a very good friend. We were both seven when we met, and now we are ninety-seven years old! And we are still in touch. Lifelong friendships can mean so much.

A girl really needs to learn how to make friends. It often seems that two friends will have a disagreement and not be able to resolve it and get back together. You need to reach the point where you can talk with each other about the things that bother you and work it all out! Develop the attitude that a person is more important than a disagreement, large or small, and remember that your friend has nice parts that you want to know about, too. You have to have the courage to say you're sorry. Learning how to say that is hard, but a friendship is too important to let a disagreement blow it all apart.

~ MARY, 97

Fitting in with the crowd is something most of us struggle with, whether we are fourteen or forty-nine. In our early teen years, however, where we belong seems to be incredibly important. Cliques and "the cool group" hold a lot of power, and girls often go to great lengths just to be like everyone else.

Every group of girls and women we met with had the same question…does anyone ever feel like they fit in? There are probably times when you wish you could reject the whole scene and just be yourself. Some of the stories ahead may sound familiar….

Fitting In

Sometimes "fitting in" gets pretty complicated at my school. Rachel decides who the most popular girl is…the one we are all supposed to be like. Who gives Rachel this power? Nobody! She just takes it! This year, Rachel decided that all the girls in my grade needed to be like Julia. Julia didn't really push to be named the Queen of Popularity, but so far she doesn't seem to mind very much. So now we are all supposed to wear the same shade of jeans that Julia wears, cut our hair to her length, wear eye makeup, be good at sports, pretty smart in math, and listen to The Beatles, Hanson, and Jewel. We are all supposed to be interested in boys now, too. In fact, Rachel spends her entire lunch period carefully matching boys in our grade with "appropriate" girls, all written out like a mad scientist in a lab!

Lots of girls actually make attempts at imitating Julia, and some succeed at it. But they get so caught up in it that they don't act real anymore. I wonder if they ever think about who they really are inside. I think I still know the real me, and I'm going to try not to forget her, even though I really want to fit in, too. But for now, I am not Julia, and I'm not the next girl who might move to the top of the popularity chart. I wear jeans that I like, my hair is the way I want it to be, and if I'd rather read a good book at recess than talk about boys or play soccer, that's okay, too.

~ NICKY, 13, JUST ME

The Clique

In my day, there was a group of girls in junior high school known as The Clique. This wasn't just a bunch of popular kids who had achieved some kind of vague recognition for being cool. This was an organized club called The Clique. I used to believe they had regular, weekly meetings to discuss their coolness, but now I think that might have been my imagination.

The members of The Clique wore a special medallion around their necks. I can still remember exactly what it looked like...a narrow rectangle of wood with a shiny brass lightning bolt on the front. The Clique girls also wore blast jackets, which were made out of lightweight, beige linen fabric, were loose-fitting, had a hood and zipped up the front. When I was honest with myself, which wasn't very often in those days, I thought those jackets were kind of ugly. But somehow, when worn by a member of The Clique, a blast jacket became immediately desirable.

Well, naturally I wanted...needed...a blast jacket more than anything else in the world. I also craved a lightning bolt medallion, but had never seen one in a store. I thought The Clique leaders might award them in some special Clique ceremony. But anyone could buy new clothes, and if I just happened to show up at school one day wearing a blast jacket, surely the other kids would recognize my coolness. I'd immediately be invited to the next Clique meeting. And then, could my lightning bolt medallion be far behind?

At home, I began to wage a long campaign to buy a blast jacket. It was similar to my previous campaign when I wanted a mohair sweater. That campaign had been successful, so I figured that nightly whining and crying might work once again. Never mind that the fuzzy, brown mohair sweater had made me look like an adolescent grizzly bear, or that it had itched me to the point of distraction. The blast jacket would be different... it would make me cool.

Unfortunately, my sensible, practical mother put her foot down before my efforts even got off the ground. I managed to drag her as far as the J.C. Penney's store, where she took a good, long look at a blast jacket. "There's nothing to it! You'll freeze to death in this thing!" (We lived in Minnesota at the time, so Mom was making a pretty good point. At least, that's what I think now that I am a Mom myself.) "Mom," I pleaded. "All the other kids have them!" My mother's mouth became a thin line on her face. "It's too expensive," she said. "Now let's go look at the long underwear." That was the end of it. I didn't get my blast jacket, and I never made it into The Clique, either.

Today my thirteen-year-old daughter is amazed that I had wanted to wear an ugly jacket just because a bunch of dumb kids were wearing them. She says it's a stupid story, and she doesn't get the point of it. She herself isn't stupid enough for that nonsense. Annie picks out clothes that are warm enough for skiing or comfortable enough for softball practice. And playing the trombone. And all the other stuff she does that has nothing to do with being cool.

Annie wouldn't wear a blast jacket if you paid her. Or a lightning bolt medallion, either. And that's the best part of the story for her and me!

~ LISA, 47, WRITER

The Geese

I would make a poor goose. "Why are we at this angle and not another?" I'd ask. I'd want to slip out of line, swoop down, and explore the lakes and hills we flew over. I'd get tired of the lines filled with geese, the honking, and the endless flapping of wings. I'd want to be alone, be quiet, have time just to think.

We are told to be like everyone else in many areas of our lives…at school, in our jobs, with friends, and with family. We are laughed at if we are different. It is easier to be just like everyone else. We learn to hide our thoughts and dreams. The world is a simpler place if no one steps out of line. Like the geese, we keep heading in the same direction. But we need to question, to look at what we've done, to see if a plan we've made is still a good idea. We don't need more people who force their beliefs on others. They would only make the whole vee of geese fly in a different direction without thinking about where they were going. What we need are people who know right from wrong, and who refuse to do the wrong thing, even if it is what everyone else is doing. We need people who are not afraid to think on their own, and to believe in what they have discovered. This kind of thinking is some of the best fun there is.

Don't just be a follower. Think!

~ Sue, 44

Different

I feel different. Different from my friends, and different from the way society wants me to be. Sometimes this is an advantage, yet other times it doesn't feel very good. But it's just how God planned it for me. God wanted me to be different. If we were all the same, then God would have probably picked one person, and everyone would act, look and be exactly like that one, appointed person. But then that person would have all the power, and might become a little greedy.

Some of the kids in my school are trying hard to look exactly like everyone else. They wear the same clothes, talk the same way, and end up looking like dumb little clones. But no matter how hard they try, they can't look alike. Some girls are more developed than others, and their body shapes are really different. I don't even have much of a chest yet, but both of my best friends wear bras. We don't look the same at all!

I think we were all meant to be different, and someday we'll be glad for this. That's what God had in mind. Trying so hard to be just like everyone else won't work. Be yourself and just have fun with who you are!

~ Chelsea, 13, proud of who I am

People sometimes try to change us, hoping to transform us into the type of friend they need or want instead of just accepting us as we are. Here are some things you might say if there is a friend in your life trying to do this....

> I wish you would accept me for who I am.
>
> I wish you would lend me a helping hand.
>
> I wish you would respect me, my color, my background.
>
> I wish you would stop living like a merry-go-round,
>
> And keep your feet on solid ground.
>
> I wish you would accept yourself.
>
> I wish you would just be you and only you.
>
> I wish you would try to understand me for who I am.
>
> —*Tiara, 14, future doctor*

When we think of peer pressure, what usually comes to mind is drinking, smoking, using drugs, or taking other risks. Peer pressure requires a decision...should I do what others want me to do, or take a different type of risk and do what I think I should do?

Dark Corners

It was early autumn, and sixth grade had just begun. The leaves were beginning to turn brilliant colors, and changes were beginning to take place within me, too. For so long I had wondered what it would be like to be a middle school student, and now that time was here. To add to my excitement, I had been invited to a party at the home of one of the "coolest" kids in my small town.

I arrived at Barb's party to join a crowd of sixth and seventh graders gathering in the garage behind her house. Music was playing, and kids were dancing and singing to the sounds of "Sugar Sugar," a song by a popular group called The Archies. A metal tub holding cans of soda was in one corner, and all of the tables were piled high with bags of chips and plates of brownies. Off in a dark corner of the garage, several kids were drinking beer that one boy had brought from home. I wondered how they would be acting later in the evening, never having been to a kids' party where drinking was going on.

I couldn't believe that I was finally part of the "in crowd"! I remember looking around at the other kids who were there, some of whom had already spent a great deal of time in the principal's office. I carefully checked out the clothes they were wearing, envying the girls with tight bell-bottom jeans.

Suddenly in the backyard, voices were getting louder and louder, and someone was beginning to yell and swear. As the crowd around the incident grew, I decided to go check it out. After all, I had been invited to be a part of this group, and I had better prove to them that I was worthy of the invitation! What I witnessed soon changed all that, however. A friend's older brother, Mike, had arrived, much to Barb's dismay. When Mike wouldn't leave as quickly as Barb wanted him to, she struck him on his back with a hammer! I was in shock! I began to imagine what other situations might develop as the evening wore on. I knew that I did not want to wait around to find out, and quietly slipped away into Barb's house to phone my mother for a ride home. I waited inside, scared to return to the backyard scene, yet worried for Mike. I was relieved to later see him and some of his friends walking home. Mike was not seriously injured.

I suppose I needed to experience first-hand what it felt like to be part of a different crowd. I am so glad to have made the choice to remain with my true friends. We may not have led exciting teenage lives, but we had fun just the same. The ironic thing about Barb is that she continues to get herself into troublesome situations to this day. I wonder how her adult years would have been if she had made some other choices about friendships back in sixth grade....

~ DEB, 39, STILL IN TOUCH WITH
SIXTH-GRADE FRIENDS

Summer in Reno

The summer after I graduated from high school, I got a job as a waitress in Reno, Nevada. There I met a woman named Ty. She had come to Reno from a small town, just like me. We were both transplanted to the bustle and the glitter, to the "darker side" of life. We were eager to be out on our own for the first time, and shared an apartment. This was the summer I "grew up."

Ty was far more experienced with life than I was. This proved true on the night she invited some friends to our apartment for a party. There was dancing and drinking, and this was my first experience with alcohol. Everyone teased me about being an eighteen-year-old who had never tried drinking before. They kept saying that everyone did it, and not wanting to look odd, I tried some beer and a shot of whiskey. I remember nothing after that except waking up to the worst headache in the world.

I decided that I didn't like being out of control, and drinking did that to me. Even if anyone teased me, I was not going to drink again. From then on at parties, I sometimes pretended to drink, but would later go to the bathroom and pour the drinks down the drain. Because most of my friends would drink until they were drunk, no one ever knew that I had tricked them. I really did grow up that summer. I began to learn to trust my own instincts.

~ DEBORAH, 48, MOTHER OF FIVE

There are times when kids do cruel things! To feel like we belong, we sometimes go to great lengths to exclude others. Secret clubs, passing notes, and gossiping on the phone are all ways of making others feel left out.

In the Club

When I was eleven, I spent a lot of time with three friends. They came up with the idea of forming a club. We were all included in the club, but other members were to be selected by us. Some kids would be accepted, while some would not. I told Mom about the club, and she told me that she did not want me to be a part of something that excluded others. When I saw my friends in school the next day, I told them the news.

Later that day, a piece of notebook paper was being passed around the classroom. When it finally reached my desk, I was horrified to read what it said. "If you hate Susie, write your name down on this paper." Everyone in the class had written his or her name down! I don't remember much between that moment and when I got home and dissolved into tears. I told Mom about it, and she called the mothers of these three friends, explaining what had happened and how much it had hurt me. (Mom usually just told me to "grin and bear it" when things like this happened!)

It was so hard to go to school the next day and face everyone! It quickly became clear that the whole class didn't really hate me, though. They felt they had to add their names to the list because these girls wanted them to. I soon discovered that I had many friends... not just those three girls.

From this incident I learned that membership in a club is not as important as loyalty or trust when it comes to friends. You can survive rejection and still feel whole. And Moms are often there for you, even though you may not always agree with them!

~ SUSIE, MOTHER OF THREE

We want to belong; we want to be "normal." It hurts to feel so different from the rest, even though others usually appreciate those things that make us each unique. This woman shares a different perspective on cliques, reminding us that it is okay to want to be a part of a group.

Belonging

Is there anything positive to say about being in a tight group of friends? After all, isn't that what a clique is? The very word sends shivers down most people's spines. Immediately, scenes of being left out fill the mind and poke at the heart. But I believe that at age thirteen, belonging is as important as eating, sleeping, and breathing!

A grouping, a gang, a club, a commune. Sisterhood, sorority, secret society. A team, a circle, the in-group, a bunch. Squad, chapter, insider, one of us. We yearn to know our place, to be there, and to know that we fit in somehow, with somebody. It won't always be this way, as soon the quest turns to striving to be different, unique, one of a kind.

So let's not forget the inner urge to be a part of the big picture. Belonging is okay, and if you think there is no room for your incredible self in an existing gaggle of girls, start your own!

~ LENA, 49, CIVIL ENGINEER

Bridge Kids

I was different from other kids. I didn't want to feel different, but there was nothing I could do about it. My Dad died when I was baby, and in the 1940s, there were very few children with no father and a working mother. I know now that I probably felt more different than I appeared to others, but for me, the differences were real!

I had many friends, but I still wasn't like all the other kids. Being "different" became "not as good as," so I worked hard to be as good as everyone else. But I never felt like I belonged anywhere. Mom told me that I was learning something very important through all this, but I still envied all those kids who seemed to fit in.

The real breakthrough came for me when I was in college, studying to become a teacher. My professor talked about ways to bring about change in the classroom and encourage growth in students. He said to look for the kids who did not belong to any particular group, but who had a variety of friends. He called these students "bridge kids," adding that there weren't many of them, but that they were the key people in the classroom who made things happen.

As I heard his words, tears began to stream down my cheeks. I had been a "bridge kid"! The weight of being different all those years finally fell away from me.

Is it all right to be different? You bet it is! Celebrate your differences and those in others, too. You just might be one of those "bridge kids" who makes things happen!

~ LINDA, 55, COUNSELOR IN
SPECIAL EDUCATION

Losing a friend is never easy, but this can happen as people change and grow in different ways. Sometimes a friendship fades out completely, but it can also rekindle itself like a fire that still has reasons to glow....

School Bus Blues

I walked by her on the school bus, glanced at her quickly, then kept walking down the narrow aisle. My nose was in the air; a slightly pained look was in my eyes. I tried to hide my true feelings and not allow my tears to flow, but while my exterior seemed calm, inside me there was a tempest at its peak. How *could* she?

We had spent countless hours confiding in each other. All of the deep, dark secrets that I had shared with her came flooding back to me. But suddenly she had decided that we weren't best friends anymore. My anger faded to fear, and I wondered if she would tell anyone those secrets. She wouldn't, would she? But she has no reason not to. She knows that I have no one else to tell her secrets to, and even if I did, no one would ever believe me.

"Nice way to start the day!," I say to myself, sarcastically. I open my notebook to begin my unfinished homework. "At least I'm learning a lot about friendships." It's not always easy, learning these hard lessons. The bus slowly turns into the school driveway, and I wonder if she and I will ever be friends again....

~ ANONYMOUS, 14

Over and over again, girls wanted to talk about what happens in their school lunchrooms! The "fitting-in drama" is performed there every day. Who sits at which table; who is in charge of the "pecking order" of popularity; who feels rejected and sits alone at a table far from the crowd. Here are some ideas from middle school girls who are trying hard to make changes in their lunchroom scene.

On finding friends in the lunchroom....

Look for someone who appears to be as insecure as you are. She may become your best "lunch bud"!

Put blinders on to those cool cliques and go for the "regular" people.

Find a friend who will table hop with you. The two of you can eat at a different table every day, or in a favorite teacher's room with a few friends.

Invite kids who are eating alone to join you. You may just make a new friend!

Turn your lunch table into a crazy quilt! Eat with kids from all different groups, and you will have a lot of fun.

Don't be afraid to look for a friend. There is someone out there just like you, in the same situation, looking for a friend, too!

Finding friends and fitting in is a lifelong task. Our situations change...new school, new place to live, new job. We change, and often need something different in our friendships. Sometimes we are lucky enough to have a friendship that will survive major changes in lifestyles and circumstances.

New Kid on the Block

I just moved into the neighborhood from out of state. Some of the kids at school tell me that I have a "funny accent," and I know I'm pretty shy. How will I ever make new friends?

I've met a few kids who are into sports. Some are into bike riding and in-line skating. Some are into *Teen* magazine, makeup, and boys. Others are into CDs, and know all the words to all the songs of the popular bands. I want to belong to one group, and came close to asking my parents to buy me the clothes and things that that group is into. But deep inside, I know that this isn't what I want. That crowd seems rowdy, confused, and more into finding trouble than I am. So I'm not going to ask my parents for those things to help me fit in, and I think it's probably the right decision.

I remember telling my friend Laura when she was going to move away that it was better to walk alone than to get involved with a group that doesn't fit with the "real you." She moved, and found some true friends. Boy, what I would give to fit right in, right now.

~ DIANNE, 15

Statistics

It's twilight in Brooklyn. A cool breeze passes over 85th Street, and I can't decide which is worse....the August humidity or the teasing, cool air. As I stand outside Baskin-Robbins, my eyes take in the usual Saturday night sights. Loud white cars with black tinted windows speed by, honking at no one in particular. To my right, my friend Jessica nudges me as we wait for our friends. They are upstairs across the street saying good night to their families. Three girls with babies already. Jessica and I stare as our friends run down the stairs, slamming the heavy wooden door behind them.

Another breeze slips by, lifting Tanya's hair. Her daughter just turned two. Who decided that Jessica and I would end up in college, and they would all be married with children by age nineteen? I know that Jessica is thinking the same thing.

Katie became a certified beautician after she dropped out of high school. I watch her long, red fingernails wave in the air as she excitedly talks to the others. We've all known each other since fourth grade, and it's still comfortable when we're together. But I can tell we're all thinking about how different our lives are now.

Lana's son Joey will be two in the fall. Lana will be twenty next month. Jess grabs my arm and throws her head back. Both are indications to leave. Instead I hold back, searching my friends' faces. Our lives at college are so different from this. We link arms and run across the street…all of us, still together, still friends.

~ OLIVIA, 21, DARK AND LOVELY

The Real You

I think that it's important to be in contact with other girls and women. It's such a relief to talk with my friends about any problem I'm having. They understand, because they're usually going through the same problems, too!

It's also important to be yourself. Believe in yourself, and be glad that you are who you are. Friends can help you see the real you, at a time when life can be so confusing.

~ ZOE, 14

Come Close,
Go Away

The Drama of Mother-Daughter Relationships

hen your life first began, you were totally dependent on your mom. You floated safely inside her. There was no way you could survive alone. She gave you life, nourished you, and then gave birth to you. But from that day on, the drama of your relationship with your mother began. This chapter gives us a glimpse of the multicolored roles that we take on as mothers and daughters throughout our lives.

Our biological mothers and other women who mother us as young children nurture, protect, and teach us. They help us become who we are. But growing up means slowly moving from dependence to independence. Separation can be confusing, and can feel like an emotional roller coaster for both moms and daughters. The "come close, go away" messages that we send each other are a frustrating but natural part of growing up. Here are some writings that describe how young women feel about their relationships with their moms.

Mommy?

Mommy? I love you because you love me and care for me and you are my safety...

Mommy? I'm older now and I have friends and fun that does not involve you, but still you are my safety...

Mommy? Now I am older still, and I stay out late and don't even want safety, so go away and leave me alone. I'm too old for mommies...

Mommy? My friends dropped me, so now I want you to help me and love me again like when I was little, because I feel like nothing...

Mommy? I have new friends, so let go of me again. I have better things to do...

Mommy? Now there are parties and drugs and danger, but you can't help me because I am too cool to talk to my mommy...

Mommy? My boyfriend dumped me and I need a hug, but not in front of the window, okay?...

Mommy? Yesterday I found myself talking to you and it was almost a little fun, so maybe today we can go somewhere. Now we are laughing and telling stories and maybe my mommy isn't as dumb as she is supposed to be. Now I think of you as my friend. How could I not have realized that until now? I think I'm too young not to have a mommy. I love you, mommy.

~ JESSICA, 14

The Beginning of Letting Go

Some days I look at my mom and I am so proud of her. My mom takes care of herself. She exercises and eats well and is a good role model for me. I know that she had a tough childhood, and she has worked hard at being a strong, independent woman. I really respect her.

It is weird, though. Even though I feel pretty close to my mom, lately there have been things that I just don't feel comfortable talking to her about. It's not that she's not willing to talk about boys or sex or decisions that I have to make about friends and stuff. She is. She's a good listener.

Some of my friends even talk to her about personal things. I just don't feel like talking to her. Sometimes I think it hurts her feelings, and I feel a little guilty.

Is this just the beginning of letting go? I hope she can understand.

~ ANONYMOUS, 15

Love Hate

I remember hating her! Absolutely hating her! I thought that she was the worst person in the world, yet I was forced to live with her. I hated the way she spoke to me, and even the way she looked at me!

One morning while we were eating breakfast, these horrible feelings of hatred arose in me because of the noises she was making while she was chewing her cereal. Suddenly and sharply I looked up at her and yelled, "Stop making those noises!" She looked at me as if I had slapped her. I felt so bad that I left the table. I hated her even more for making me feel bad.

Looking back, I wonder how I could have had such feelings of hatred towards the very person who gave me my life. It brings tears to my eyes to realize the way that I felt about my mother back then. Now she is one of my greatest friends and role models. Time sure changes things....

~ JULIE, 27

NEVER A MOTHERLESS CHILD

You stand by my side,

You watch me grow.

I love you...that you should know.

You helped me realize the wrong,

But I didn't listen and found out the hard way.

It's a fact.

You make a point with what you say.

Mom, you are like a lot of others

But nothing like the careless mothers.

I wish we could find a place where we could both unwind.

It's lost time we need to find.

I want to be able to talk in a reasonable tone,

To listen to each other, so we're not alone.

I've cried on your shoulder and caused you pain.

Sometimes I wonder if we are both insane.

Please hear me.

It's taking time.

But some day we will be able to understand each other,

I hope to be able to get along with you, Mother.

It is a relationship.

A two-way street.

But we can walk alone

On our own two feet.

~Sarah, 16, teenage mom

Fog

I went for a walk with my dog, Garnet, this morning. The ground is covered with five inches of wet snow. It is cloudy, but the air is warm. This feels strange for December; a menthol kind of feeling...hot and cold at the same time. A thick fog has settled where the warm air meets the cold snow. The mist swirls over the snow, pushed around by a gentle breeze that is blowing off the lake.

This strange winter scene is like my mom and me these days. She is the wet, heavy snow that has made its journey down to earth. Now it lies still and heavy on the ground. I am the warm December air, a little out of place, and very different from the snow. Together we create a foggy confusion that makes it hard for us to understand each other. She doesn't see me, and I can barely see her through this fog. But I know she's there.

When I step back from all of this, it is actually beautiful, in an eerie sort of way. The mist is magical and unpredictable. It is a natural result of the warm air and the cold snow coming together. Maybe the confusion between my mom and me is natural, too. Maybe if we keep trying to reach out to each other, we can connect in all of this fog.

~ ANONYMOUS, 16

The love that a mother has for a child is deep and primitive, full of protective instincts. But as little girls grow into young women, mothers have to learn how to express their love in new ways. As Moms, we learn to love by letting go, but try to be close when our daughters need us.

The Key Is in the Caring

I recently discovered a letter that my mother wrote to my sister and me twenty years ago. Oddly enough, I don't remember it being significant to me as a young teenager. My friendships were the biggest part of my life then. On some level, however, I knew that the letter was important enough to tuck away. I uncover it only now, as a mother of two young girls who are about to take off on their own journeys into womanhood.

I always knew that my mother was there for me. Even though I naturally rejected her involvement in my life at times, I quietly appreciated her commitment to my growth.

Now I am faced with the very same job that my mother had. I was lucky to have had a mother who was a wise woman…caring, open, and supportive, all necessary ingredients for nurturing a young woman. I am eternally grateful for the ways in which she modeled a healthy mother-daughter relationship.

~ KAREN, 34, MOTHER

This is the beginning of the letter that Karen tucked away twenty years ago for safekeeping....

Dear Karen and Amy,

I feel like our talks are open, no matter how much it hurts sometimes. I know that real growth only occurs when a parent can be fully engaged with a kid's mind, body, and soul. The key is in the caring...to do whatever is needed, whether it seems hard or feels supportive. I try to give you room to make mistakes and pick up the pieces. Sometimes my demands and expectations seem unrealistic to you, but please know that even though you may feel this, they are shared in love and concern for the emergence of healthy, well-adjusted kids who feel pride in themselves and in their decisions.

You are both on the right track to knowing where you are going, but neither one of you has made your last mistake. Believe me, I surely haven't either! I know that the positive qualities you have developed as young girls will emerge at the forefront as you step towards womanhood....

~ MOM

Significant events mark when we move from one part of our lives to another. We let go of the past and step into the future. This is called a rite of passage. Graduations, bat mitzvah, confirmation, a girl's first period, and significant birthdays are all rites of passage that we celebrate in this culture, but there are many other ways that you can intentionally mark moving from one stage of your life to another. Some of these ideas appear in other chapters of this book.

For mothers and daughters, rites of passage are bittersweet. Our joy is mixed with a tinge of sadness. We reflect on what was, realize what is, and imagine the future. We let go. We step forward. We trust in what lies ahead. It may seem like your parents go a little overboard with all of this sometimes, but remember…they gave birth to you, and your growing is their growing, too.

Eighth Grade Graduation

My daughter graduated from eighth grade this week. I sat on the bleachers in her middle school gym next to hundreds of other parents so packed in on that hot June evening that we could see our body moisture fog the air. As the kids marched into the school, the collective lumps in the parents' throats seemed more noticeable than the heat. We, I expect, were all thinking the same thought: Where did the time go?

With the intensity of a single mom, I watched my daughter march in. Her brother and I have been all she has had since she was eight and her father died suddenly, leaving us to a world we hardly recognized. I've watched my daughter progress from a bubbly toddler, grinning from the driver's seat of her father's tractor, to a frozen eight-year-old, holding onto whatever version of reality would preserve her, to a questioning twelve-year-old, and now to a budding young woman, ready to take on the world.

But not in a dress. Meli hates dresses, especially those frilly dresses with lace and ruffles. Some of the other girls wore long satin gowns, others sophisticated, black slinky numbers with cut-out shoulders, but Meli wore a brightly-colored cotton romper of mine. She looked confident and beautiful, with that combination of sweetness and grace that fourteen-year-old girls have. Meli has been lucky. She never went through that awkward stage that so many teenagers experience when they are in constant warfare with their bodies. Meli and her body were made for each other. She is small and slim, but strong. A tomboy, which is not surprising, since she and her brother have either been inseparable or fighting all her life. The boys in her class stay clear of Meli when they are in the mood to tease someone, because she can lick any one of them, and they know it! I don't protest the feistiness in her. I am also the sister of an older brother who taught me how to be tough.

Now, as I watch her standing when her name is called, I see a smirk on her face at the fuss we adults make over rites of passage. I also see a confident girl ready to leave middle school and make her way through the vast halls and even vaster emotional labyrinths of high school. Yet I also hear her quiet voice wisely asking if everything changes when you get to high school. Do friendships break up? Do people change forever? Will her small circle of buddies crack at the center when faced with drugs, alcohol, older men? She knows that Mom can't answer all of the questions, fix all of the problems. She learned that at eight when her exuberant father became ashes in a box. But she asks me these things anyway because she is my daughter and I am the hub of our little family wheel.

Sometimes I look at her as if she is not my daughter and wonder what kind of person she will be. This often happens as I watch her running in her track meets. Cross- country is especially grueling. She runs in rain, mud, up hills, over rocks, down mudslides. She runs with impeccable posture… head up, chin out, her long brown hair sailing behind her, the only sign of strain her red cheeks. When she crosses the finish line, she does not collapse on the ground as some runners do, but leans over, hands on her knees, breathing quietly. I watch her, this determined young woman who looks so much like her father. I weep, realizing that I have no idea who she will become. She has been on loan to me for a few years, but soon she will go off into her life. I am grateful for my time with her and just hope that when the moment comes for her to leave, she, and I, will be ready.

~ MARIAN, 44

The "letting go" between a mother and a daughter happens many times during our lives. When this woman's mother moved away, she finally felt the reality of separation.

So It Goes

Sometimes it feels as though I didn't really connect with my mom until I was middle-aged. Although we had been close for years, it was right before she got the crazy notion to run off to Alaska with my dad that we found a common ground.

It's not that I thought that she didn't deserve a life of her own. After all, I had earned one. But this was my mother! What was she thinking? Who would dry my tears and help me fight my dragons? Who would walk with me in the woods and help me put myself back together again? And why hadn't I found her sooner? If only I had known that she would turn out to be my best friend.

I put Mom to the test many times over the years. Sometimes I didn't know how I would survive. Now I wonder how she did. After raising three sons of my own and nurturing three grandchildren, I know that I'm not nearly as tough as she is.

I was about to find out what it was like to stand on my own two feet. "She's only a phone call away," I was told. But with Mom gone, my haven in the woods where I used to walk and feel the earth and sky was gone, too. It just wasn't the same.

In my mind I kept hearing: "Pick yourself up. Find your backbone and learn to trust in yourself. It's your turn to be in charge, to pull the family together. Holidays and birthdays, all of the family events, are yours to coordinate now, just like Mom did..." Yeah, right! Mom made it all seem effortless, this business of being the Center of the Universe.

I have stumbled and stood tall. I will be forever grateful for the strength and love my mother has given me to enjoy and to pass along. I see her in myself every day, in the little things...the way I love my grand-daughters, and in the understanding I have with my own grown children. I guess I'll be all right. I am onto the business of living. And so it goes....

~ KATHI, 46, DAUGHTER, MOTHER, GRANDMOTHER

As a teenager, your relationship with your parents can be really challenging. It's not always easy to find ways to be understood. Don't forget that the stuff you are going through may be pushing your parents' buttons. They were once teenagers, too, and may have their own unfinished, adolescent strug-gles. It's their job to deal with their feelings, and it's your job to find effective ways to communicate to them what is going on for you. Here are some thoughts that girls have shared with their parents in order to feel more understood....

"If you want me to be open and talk with you, then be willing to listen without judgment. I need someone to listen and accept me. Don't always tell me what I did wrong or what I should think. I will learn from my own mistakes if you give me a chance."

"If you want me to be happy, just telling me to be happy won't work! Show me how much you love me. Spend time with me."

"If you tell me that I can make a decision, then support me in whatever decision I make. Don't keep second-guessing me or I will grow up struggling with even the simplest choices."

"If you want me to think for myself and not worry about what other people think about me, then don't always be worried about what other people think of you. Be yourself if you want me to be myself!"

"If you want me to have a loving relationship, show me how it is done. Don't be afraid to hold hands with Dad, kiss each other, and show affection in front of me. Otherwise, when you tell me someday to go ahead and hold my boyfriend's hand, I will be uncomfortable to show affection in front of others."

"If you are upset about something in your own life, don't take it out on me. Do something about it. Listen to your own advice."

"If you want me to value our family, then find ways to make it seem important and create some happy memories. Make sure we spend some time all together."

"If you make a mistake or a bad decision, tell me about it. I can learn from your experiences."

"I am not you, or Dad, or my brother or sister. See me for who I am."

"If it's too hard for you to talk to me about some of the stuff that I am dealing with, then help me find someone who can."

Spend some time thinking about what would help you and your mom communicate in a healthy way. It takes two of you to have a relationship, and your mom doesn't always have the answers. Be brave enough to share your suggestions.

There still may be times when it's hard to keep your voice with your parents....

My Daughter's Decision, Not Mine

When I was in sixth grade, I began to develop breasts, and I was uncomfortable wearing just my regular shirt. I was sure I needed a bra. My mom was sure that I didn't. When I first asked her about it, she reached up, felt my breasts, and said, "You don't need a bra yet."

I remember running to my room, crying. I wasn't only upset because she said "no." I was upset because she had put her hand on my breast. I'm sure she didn't think twice about it, but today it still troubles me to think about how she invaded my privacy. Instead of becoming a time that brought me closer to my mom and helped me feel good about my changing body, I felt alone, angry at her for feeling my breast, and angry at myself for not stopping her. I was left with the lasting impression that my opinion didn't matter, even about my own body.

Now I am a mom. When my oldest daughter began to develop breasts, she and I went together to buy her some bras. I wanted her to have a few bras to wear when she felt that she wanted to or needed to. The decision was hers, not mine. It's her body. She knew that she had my blessing when she was ready.

~ ANONYMOUS, 35

Like a Yo-Yo

I remember asking my mother how long it would take me to become an adolescent. She explained that usually "adolescent" meant turning thirteen. I asked her if it was really true that I had to become an adolescent before I could be an adult. Mom replied that this was indeed a fact…one had to come before the other. Rolling my eyes and sighing, I shook my head in disbelief. My impatience was showing, and Mom then asked me why I was in such a hurry to grow up. I remember responding, "Because I've got a lot of things to do with my life!"

Ages ten, eleven, twelve…I felt like I had no identity. I wasn't really a child, but I wasn't an adolescent either, according to my mother. Privileges and responsibilities came and went without anyone explaining why. One minute I was told that I had to do certain household chores or babysitting because I was "almost grown." The next minute, they told me I couldn't do something, like go to the movies with my friends, because I was "not old enough." Who was in charge of all this changing, anyway? I felt like a yo-yo on a short string, but eventually it became clear to me just who I was and what it meant to truly be an adolescent.

If you have any questions, ask someone about them. Ask a neighbor, a teacher, ask your best friend's mother if you can't ask your own mother what's going on. Keep asking until you get the answers you need.

~ Luisah, 50

Mothers, grandmothers, aunts, teachers, and older female friends can all nurture and guide us as young women. Most women feel a "mothering instinct" in some way. They can share the wisdom of a mother, even if they are not mothers themselves. The following stories are about ways that girls can connect with female role models when their own moms aren't emotionally or physically available.

I Knew You Could Do It!

When I was really young, my mom was hardly ever around because she was always working on the farm. Both of my grandmothers died before I was eight years old. I never had a chance to know them, but I was lucky enough to have a neighbor named Anna who treated me just like her granddaughter. She was single and never had any children of her own, but I always felt like we were related somehow. She led a very interesting life, traveled all over the world, and would talk to me in French and German. I can still remember the cream cheese and cucumber sandwiches she would make for me on rainy summer afternoons.

I moved away from the town where Anna lived when I was in seventh grade. We wrote letters back and forth for several years, but by the time I was a sophomore in high school, we had lost touch with each other.

Last June I graduated from high school. The day before graduation, a small package arrived at my door with no return address. I opened the box, and it was from Anna. The dark blue velvet case held a beautiful silver bracelet, just like one she used to wear. The card simply read, "I knew you could do it. Love you, Anna." Tears of gratitude filled my eyes.

Now I am in my first year of college. I am meeting tons of people at school and in the community where I live. Looking back, I realize what a gift my relationship with Anna was. She was there when I really needed her. She was a mentor, a friend, a great listener, and she believed in me.

Many women in the world have the nurturing energy of a mother or grandmother. As you become a woman, look for an "Anna" in your life.

She may be a relative, your neighbor, a teacher, or a woman you meet on the street. But her stories and ideas may plant seeds in you that will grow in time.

~ Anna's friend, 18

Second Chances

My mother died of leukemia when I was five years old. It seems that my entire life has revolved around losing her and growing up without a mom. I didn't allow anyone else into my life who might betray her memory. From the time I was twelve or thirteen, every year on her birthday and on the anniversary of her death, I would get very upset. I used these days to mourn her rather than to celebrate her life. I would sit alone in a dark room, light candles, listen to sad music, and stare at photographs of her. Not only did this affect me, but it impacted everyone around me. I put my stepmother through years of pain because I was unable to let go of my mother's memory. My father was trying to move on with his life, but I constantly mentioned my mother's name and tried to hold him back.

I needed my mother to help me grow up. I didn't think that anyone else on earth could teach me how to become a woman because only *she* was my biological mother. I felt guilty whenever I tried to love my stepmother or other women in my life, even though my own mother would have wanted me to share a mother-daughter relationship with someone. I knew in my heart that my mother could never be replaced. My stepmother was not trying to replace her; she simply wanted to be my friend.

I have learned one lesson from all of this…a mother's bond with a child will always survive. There will always be a connection. If you have the chance to create a special relationship with someone else who can serve as a positive role model and encourage you along life's path, grab it! If you push them away enough times, you may not get another chance.

I was twenty-two before I realized that I had lost something that could have been wonderful with my stepmother. Now I am ready to have a relationship with her. Slowly, my dad and I are developing a special bond that was never a part of our past, and I think it will happen with my step-mother, too.

~ NEILLE, 22

There are many women in the world open and ready to share their mother wisdom with you. Watch and wait. Your next door neighbor, a teacher, or a woman you meet in the park someday may have a piece of wisdom that you need!

Mother Wisdom

To the daughter I will never have,

I am writing to you to share some of the mother wisdom deep within me. I am not able to talk to you about these things because, although I have a beautiful son, I have no daughter to share the feminine wisdom that has been given to me by the women in my life. Whenever I see a young girl, I think of you. I imagine who you might have been. I promise to share these thoughts with the young women I meet along the way.

My wise mother taught me the power of nurturing our creativity. She taught me late in her life that I shouldn't wait for perfection, because we never know how long we have upon the earth. As women, we are caretakers, and it is one of the finest traits we possess. One warning…don't forget to take care of *yourself*. A woman who only cares for others may find herself drowning if she doesn't take time for herself.

My grandmothers taught me about living life to the fullest. Be curious and never stop asking questions until you understand. Take risks, travel, and seek education. Life is an adventure!

Your strength as a woman can lie in your desire to give something back to the world, even when the world doesn't seem to be giving to you. Unselfishness and giving without expectation are expressions of love.

Remember the importance of your family stories...not just the happy, joyful ones, but the dark and tragic ones too. We learn from each other's experiences. Share your story so that you may learn from the telling and others can learn from you.

Now I am the matriarch of the family. The others have died and their work is done. It's up to me now to help you feel some connection to the women who came before you in this world. When I see you in the face of a young girl on the street, at work, at church, or in my family, I will tell you my story. I will be ready.

~ SALLY, 41

Grandmothers play a special role in our lives when we are becoming women. Since we usually don't live with them every day, we don't worry quite as much about upsetting them or hurting their feelings. Sometimes it's easier to listen to the wisdom of a grandma....

Winonah

I visited my grandmother, Winonah, only four or five times in my childhood, but whenever I did, she would sit me on her lap. She always wore purple, and always smelled of lavender. In those quiet moments, she would remind me, "Tessie, security is knowing that we have none." She presented these words to me as Great Truth, quietly, peacefully, but powerfully. Then she would pat me on the leg.

I'm sure she must have said other things to me, too, but these words made a huge impression on me, even though I didn't know what they meant until I was much older.

~ TESS, 46, THERAPIST,
MOTHER OF TWO SONS

How I Learned to Knit

I don't know exactly when I started knitting, but I can tell you how it started. I was visiting my grandmother. Gramma Ginny was always knitting. She even had knitting needles in her kitchen drawer. One day I was playing with yarn and needles when Gramma Ginny came up from behind me. I jumped.

"What are you doing?" she asked.

I said, "I'm trying to figure out how to knit."

"Would you like me to teach you?" she asked gently.

I responded quickly, "Oh, could you?" And she did.

Gramma Ginny was so kind, patient and loving. She was always calm and relaxed when she was knitting, and it was a pleasure to learn from a woman who was so talented. Knitting was her passion. She refused to do dishes more than once a day. She always said it wasted time, energy, and water. And besides, it kept you from knitting!

What does all this have to do with becoming a woman? This is a story of selfless love; a story of a time when I was shown special attention at an important moment in my journey towards womanhood. Gramma Ginny took the time to teach me a craft that I have been proud of my whole life. I have been knitting for over thirty years. Now it is one of my passions.

Gramma Ginny gave me a special gift. Look for women who can share their gifts with you.

~ DARYL, 44,
SINGLE MOTHER OF TWO GIRLS

A mother's love has many faces. A daughter's love is ever changing. May we always stay open to each other, learn from our mistakes, and help each other grow into the women we want to be.

FOR MY DAUGHTER AT NINETEEN

My daughter's eyes are gray as the lake on a cloudy day,
or green as the moss in the deep wood.
Her brown hair shimmers in the sun.
She is very dear to me.

I used to pray:
"Lord, hold her in the palm of your hand.
Keep her from harm. She feels so much!"
But life is not like that, and rightly so, perhaps.

So, now I pray:
"Give her strength to meet the needs of every day,
and the courage to work her dreams.
Send her a Love
that holds her close yet sets her free!"

Growing up is very hard
for Mothers, too.

~Jean, 50

A MOTHER'S LOVE

Her wisdom is my wisdom,

Her love can be my love to share,

And her story is my story,

A story that's carried on

By so many women who care,

And passed down forever by granddaughters everywhere.

~Deb, 42, songwriter

So What's the Big Deal?

The Meaning of Menstruation

o, what's the big deal?" We hear this a lot when we bring up the topic of menstruation with teenage girls. When we really listen, we understand that the words also mean, "Stop making such a big fuss about all of this." "I really don't want to talk about it." "This is too embarrassing." The shame that has been laid upon generations of women regarding menstruation can be heard in these comments. When we get beyond the embarrassment, it becomes clear that most of us do have a desire to find some meaning in the rhythmic cycles of our bodies. We want to know what the "big deal" is, but in a way that fits for each of us.

There are as many ways to view menstruation as there are women in this world. Family traditions, religions, and cultures all shape our perceptions. In recent years, some of the stigma that has burdened our experiences has broken down. However, we still have a long way to go to educate ourselves about the biological, emotional, and spiritual aspects of menstruating. Sometimes the very things that are messy, uncomfortable, and painful can also bring meaning, connection, and new life to this world. Let's remind each other that menstruation is one of the awesome and unique parts of being a woman.

Menstruation Means...

Menstruation means growing up. When you start menstruating, you are beginning to become a woman.

When I think about getting my period, I feel a little nervous. Once a year, the school nurse comes in to talk to our class about puberty. That's when a lot of people start laughing. I do feel a little embarrassed, but I think we all need to learn about puberty and the changes our bodies are going through.

If you didn't have a chance to learn the facts, imagine what you would think when all of the changes of puberty started happening to you!

~ ANONYMOUS, 10

RHYTHM OF WOMEN

When it happened the first time,

It seemed like a dream.

Light pink stain on toilet paper,

Hug from Mom, flower from Dad,

Over and done with in two days.

No big deal.

But when it happened again the next month,

Reality hit.

Truth squeezed into my body with each little cramp.

I really was becoming a woman.

In the months that followed, everything seemed so new.

Sharing stories of first periods,

Offering sympathy when my friend had cramps,

Teaching my sister about tampons.

It made me feel part of something...

A rhythm of women, bleeding together, bringing life to this world.

~almost a woman, 16

In some of the writing groups we have held, girls and women were asked what menstruation meant to them. Here are some of the things they shared....

What Does Menstruation Mean to You?

"Turning from a girl into a woman." —age 11

"Really bad cramps." —age 13

"Being moody." —age 12

"Something else to worry about." —age 14

"Cleansing. I know what time of the month it is!"
    —age 36

"I'm finished menstruating, and I miss it sometimes!"
    —age 53

"Being part of a cycle." —age 34

"A mess!" —age 17

"The ability to have children, nurse babies, mother."
    —age 41

"I am becoming a woman." —age 14

"That I'd better be sure to have birth control if I am going to have intercourse." —age 17

"PMS, dropping stuff, feeling fat. Sweet relief when I actually get my period." —age 39

"That I am not pregnant!" —age 27

"That I am connected to all women. I can't believe it when all of the women in my dorm get their periods on the same day. Amazing!" —age 20

Understanding the meaning that menstruation has for each of us begins with reflecting upon our own experience, then sharing our stories with other girls and women. The following pages are filled with "first period stories." Some are funny, while some are far from humorous. Regardless, these early experiences can shape our overall view of menstruation.

Announcement at the Mall

We all have our stories about our first periods. I will never forget mine for as long as I live. I was at the mall shopping with my mother. I was in the dressing room and Mom was waiting outside, bugging me to see what I was trying on. When I opened the door and whispered to her that I was bleeding, she suppressed her excitement slightly, then quickly ran to another store to get me some pads. How mortifying! Standing in a dressing room, waiting for your mom to get you feminine hygiene products. But that wasn't the worst part!

As we were leaving the mall, we ran into one of my mother's friends. Of course, Mom had to announce, "Jennifer just got her period for the first time!" I was never so embarrassed in all of my life. My mother proceeded to announce my "entry into womanhood" to everyone she talked to. She probably would have run an ad in the local newspaper if she could have!

To top it off, my older stepsister was furious because I had gotten my period before she did. As far as I was concerned, she could have it! Cramps, not being able to swim, bulky pads that made you feel like there was a quilt in your underwear...no thanks!

At first I was embarrassed about having my period. However, as I became more comfortable with my new status and learned how wonderful tampons were, I realized that there was nothing to be embarrassed about. I won't deny that there were times when I felt that having my period was a nuisance, like when I was going to the beach, or when I just didn't feel like dealing with the whole thing. But I have also felt amazed by the miracle of our bodies. Menstruation is a truly phenomenal cycle of nature that connects all women.

I can now look back on my first period and smile. I am no longer embarrassed about menstruation. In fact, I was delighted to discover that the best way to get rid of an annoying boy is to launch into an in-depth discussion about the female menstrual cycle! I have come to realize that while society sometimes makes menstruation seem dirty and taboo, there is nothing wrong with us.

I know that one day I will celebrate my passage into menopause just as I endured my passage through puberty. I also know that our lives are all about cycles and changes. I will not let society tell me what is right and what is wrong. I will celebrate my life as I know nature intended.

~ JENNIFER, 22, STUDENT

Today You Are a Woman

There I was, dressed in my can-can slips, hot-starched and ironed under a spotless dress. I was the kind of little black girl who loved to dress up, but also enjoyed fishing, hanging from the willow tree, and shooting marbles with the boys. On this day I was just about to win another cat-eye marble when my mother called out, "Heifer, come on in here!" I couldn't imagine what I had done to be called "heifer." A heifer is a grown-up female cow. I hadn't stolen anything, the dishes were washed, and my homework was done. I got up from my squatting position and went into the house.

Momma paraded me to the bathroom, stopping only to reach into the mysterious box she kept in the hall closet. She pulled out a sanitary napkin and an elastic belt with metal clamps. Momma handed me these things, pushed me into the bathroom and said, "Do what you supposed to do!"

What was I supposed to do? I stood there looking at the napkin and the belt and then I remembered. There had been rumors among the girls at school that something went on underneath big girls' dresses that didn't go on under mine. An older girl had told me that it would happen to me some day, but I doubted it.

Now, at ten years old, it was happening to me. Nervously, I pulled my white shorts down and found myself soaked in red. Then I remembered all of the rumors…this was going to hurt, it was going to happen to me for a long time. It would make me sick.

I attached the pad to the belt, and stepped into the contraption like a pair of pants. I wrapped a towel around my bottom and rinsed the rich red stains from my clothing. In fear, I put on a new pair of shorts and went back outside.

I tried hard to act as if nothing had happened.

During the next few weeks I asked for explanations about what was happening to me. The only thing I heard was, "You are a woman now."

How on earth could I be a woman now? What happened to being a girl? What happened to adolescence? Excuse me? I was a woman? What exactly did that mean?

It meant lots of warnings: "Don't take a tub bath or wash your hair when it's that time." "Don't climb trees." "Don't wear light colors." "If you don't stop playing with the little boys you'll get pregnant." It was all very confusing and scary.

I wish that I'd had a community of women back then to help me understand what was happening to my body and my mind. I wish there had been some kind of school or community program to help me process the changes. I really could have used an honest conversation about the meaning of menstruation and womanhood. I might have listened.

Because of my own experiences, I have learned to listen to young women when they talk. We must begin to honor this process of becoming a woman.

~ LUISAH, 50

I was thirteen when I first got my period. I had been babysitting for a young couple who stayed out very late that night. All through the evening and into the night, painful cramps came and went. I was bewildered and frightened and wondered if I was sick. I waited anxiously for the parents to come back. It was 2:00 A.M. when they finally took me home. I entered my house quietly and got ready for bed. When I went to the bathroom, I saw bright red blood in my underwear. I stood and stared for a long time, transfixed. It was exciting, but I still felt scared.

I woke up my older sister and showed her my underwear. She seemed as amazed as I was, but took charge in a wonderful way. She got up and showed me how to use sanitary napkins and talked to me in a loving voice.

Then the best moment came. She told me that it was a very special night in my life and that I should sleep with her. All night long she held me in her arms, and during that quiet and sleepless night, I felt the stirrings of the woman inside of me. I felt the blood flowing from my body, and felt safe, loved, and honored by my sister.

Even though there was a lot of abuse and violence in my family, some things turned out just right.

~ TESS, 46, THERAPIST,
MOTHER OF TWO SONS

Sometimes the "perfect moment" for you to talk about menstruation is not the right time for your mother. (It also works the other way around…you may not feel ready to hear what your mother wants to share!) In this story, a young French girl realizes that such a moment has passed.

Naiveté

One day when I was nine years old, I went for a walk in my very small French village and met my neighbor. She was squatting with her skirts gathered above her knees as she tended to the needs of her toddler. I couldn't help but catch a glimpse of her underwear, and I saw that they were soaked with blood. I ran home and told the story to my mother and grandmother, who were mending some clothes by the kitchen window. To my dismay, they laughed uncontrollably at my story. Between bursts of laughter, they told me that I must have been dreaming…the underwear was simply stained. I repeated my story, but they kept on laughing.

I felt confused and misunderstood. At that time in France, talking about anything to do with the genital area or bodily functions was taboo. We never discussed it again. Looking back, I now see that this would have been the perfect opportunity for my elders to teach me about menstruation.

~ NADINE, 39, MOTHER OF THREE

Leeches!

It all happened shortly after I had gotten my first period. I was working at a camp for girls in New Hampshire, and enjoyed swimming in the beautiful lake. About halfway through the season, the lake was besieged by leeches. Everyone seemed to delight in relating the latest gruesome tales of campers who had emerged from the lake with leeches fastened to their bodies, blood dripping freely. The only thing that killed the leeches was salt.

One day I went swimming and was horrified when I changed back into my clothes and saw blood dripping down my inner thigh. "Leeches!" I exclaimed to my sister. We ran to the kitchen, and I frantically started throwing salt in the area of my private parts. In the midst of all the panic, my sister gently said, "Wasn't it about this time last month when you got your period?"

I stopped and thought for a second. Ah! She was right! She still reminds me of this story today!

~ ANNE, 46

A girl's first period usually arrives between the ages of eleven and fourteen, but it can also show up a lot earlier or much later. You may be at the older end of the spectrum, waiting and wondering when your period will begin, while all of your friends have already been menstruating for years. Maybe you were the first of your friends to experience this, and now feel out of place because no one else really understands what it's all about.

No Period, Period.

My friend Margaret's big sister didn't get her period until she was seventeen. She was a senior, so I was afraid to ask her about it. I was fifteen and desperate. No breasts, no pubic hair. No period, period. I pretended to have cramps, carried pads and the other paraphernalia of puberty, and lived in constant fear of being exposed for the impostor that I was. I stuffed my bra with toilet paper and smiled knowingly during "girl-talk." I hid my growing panic that I was a freak. I would be the only girl who never physically matured into a woman.

Sixteen changed all that. My period came. But large breasts and body confidence did not come with the package. Surprise, surprise....

~ REBECCA, 49

Not Ready

I was nine when I got my period for the very first time. Only nine. I still felt like a girl in every way, and suddenly there was this part of me that said, "You are a woman now." I told my mom, but nobody else. My best friend doesn't even know! I really don't like this at all, and it bugs me when I hear other girls wishing they had it.

~ MARTA, 11

When You Don't Menstruate

Menstruation is a very integral part of womanhood, but it is important to know that there are some women who never menstruate. I have many medical problems that interfere with my ability to ovulate, menstruate, or bear children. As a teenager, I often pretended that I had my period just to fit in. I even remember buying tampons when I was downtown with some friends, just so they would think that I was "normal." After many years of wrestling with my feelings of loss about my infertility and my perceptions about my own femininity, I have come to see that my feminine energy is just as deep as any other woman's. I simply need to remind myself of that fact since I don't have the monthly blessing of a moon cycle to help me remember that I *am* a woman.

~ ANONYMOUS, 20

The following are examples of simple celebrations and rituals that families have either created or passed down from generation to generation as ways to celebrate a girl's first menstruation. You may want to work with your family or friends to elaborate on an idea you find here, creating a celebration of your own menarche.

Celebrations and Rituals

"When I got my first period, I remember my father coming home with a beautiful yellow rose. There were not a lot of words shared, just a knowing glance and a warm hug."

"My mother and older sister gave me a bracelet when my period first started. It was engraved with a leaf design to symbolize new life, since I had joined the sisterhood of women who could bring new life into the world. The bracelet and blessings were passed on to my daughter when she joined the sisterhood."

"When I first started menstruating, my mother and father drew a hot bath for me. There were candles and music, and time for me to be alone."

"In our family, when a girl first gets her period, she goes with our mom and picks out a new outfit."

"My mother gathered a circle of her closest friends together at our home one night. By candlelight, each woman shared what it meant to her be a woman."

"I finally got to pierce my ears!"

"My mom wrote me a beautiful story about when a girl becomes a woman. I will keep it and give it to my daughter some day."

"In Puerto Rico, when a girl begins menstruating, everyone says, "The rooster has crowed!" It means, "It's a new day. A girl has become a woman.""

"My mother gave me a shawl that had belonged to my great-grandmother."

"My parents never really acknowledged my passage from girlhood into womanhood, so when I went off to college, my friends and I created our own ceremony."

"My aunt gave me a little leather pouch that I sometimes wear around my neck. Inside it are things that are special to just me, and it reminds me of who I am."

On the pages that follow, several women explore more deeply the meaning that menstruation has in their lives...

Why Is It Such a Big Deal?

For most of my life, menstruation was a big deal only because it meant physical discomfort and inconvenience. In my thirties, I began to notice the recurring pattern of frustration, impatience, and irritation with others before my period started; typical PMS symptoms. After attending a workshop with Tamara Slayton, the founder of the Menstrual Health Foundation, I began to look at my cycle in a new way.

As women, we experience a natural cycle. It is guided by the rhythms in our bodies, in nature, and in each other. I now realize that as menstruation draws near, this rhythm calls me inward to consider the aspects of my life that are not working. It is a time to look at the dark parts of my soul and to face the negativity that I hold onto. It is usually not an easy time for me, because I resist taking the time to truly be just me.

It is important for us to stop and listen. By choosing to be open and receptive in silence, we not only begin to heal ourselves, but we also gain wisdom from the spiritual world. I believe that our collective work as women is to try to change the world with our love. We are given the opportunity every month to receive strength and direction for this task. A big deal? You bet it is!

~ BEVERLY, 40, WIFE, MOTHER, MUSIC TEACHER

Paper or Plastic?

Standing at the end of the thirty-foot feminine hygiene aisle at my local grocery store, I am overwhelmed. Super, slender, self-adhesive, mini, maxi, deodorant, pink, blue, biodegradable, all-natural, washable, flushable, junior, plastic, portable, stay-free pads. Whew! I have a lot of choices, and I am...thankful.

As you become a woman, you have many choices about how to care for your body and how you view menstruation. Some of us are fortunate to be born into families or communities that see menstruation in a way that fits for us. But if you were not, it is important to remember that there are at least as many ways to learn about, experience, and celebrate your first period as there are feminine hygiene products at your local grocery store.

~ BUNNY, 39

Mother Material

Menstruation is a big deal for a lot of reasons. It means that you are now "mother material." For the first time in your life, you are physically able to make a baby, and that is a big responsibility. When you begin to menstruate, you can begin to take charge of your own body and your life in new ways.

I was shocked when in ninth grade, my teacher passed out information about Planned Parenthood. I remember thinking, "Who is *planning* to be a parent now?" The answer is that probably none of my school friends had thought anything about it. Maybe that's why a couple of them were pregnant at thirteen. Remember, you *can* make adult decisions about your body.

~ ANDREA, 30, SWITZERLAND

Back Down to Earth

I appreciate my menstrual cycle because it keeps me in touch with my body. Sometimes I fly around in my hectic life, ignoring the internal, physical reality of this body that I live in. Then in a split second, a red spot on my underwear reminds me that I am *not* in control of everything. I am a female animal with a natural, internal rhythm more powerful than my date book filled with appointments. My menstrual cycle brings me back down to earth.

~ ANONYMOUS, 38

Here is a collection of short quotes reflecting the more humorous side to this whole business of menstruation. You may find that keeping your sense of humor really helps ease the discomfort that menstruation can sometimes bring....

The Lighter Side

"I remember asking my Mom if nuns got periods, too."

"I'll never forget the day I went into my daughter's room and saw mini pads stuck inside her sneakers.

Later, I discovered that she thought they were deodorant inserts for shoes."

"I have a friend who dresses up like PMS every Halloween. She even wears tampons for earrings!"

"Once when I saw a quote on a box of maxi pads that said, 'Now with more adhesive,' I asked my mom, 'Doesn't that hurt when you pull it off?' I thought you stuck the pad right to your body! Mom gently explained the proper way to use them."

"I have a male friend who was in a coed health class in fifth grade. The boys and the girls all heard the 'Getting Your Period' lecture together. Almost thirty years later, my friend finally disclosed a long-held secret. He had been really worried when he still hadn't gotten his period by age fourteen!"

"The first time I ever tried to use a tampon, I went through an entire box just trying to get one in."

"I used to think getting your period meant that you bled constantly for five days straight! No stopping; just bleeding all the time. I wondered how I was supposed to sleep at night, and how I would ever stop this wild flow long enough to change my pad. Your mind can really wander when you don't have the facts straight!"

More Than You Learned in Health Class

Sexuality, Sensuality, and First Loves

here is more to the topic of sex than you've learned in health class…more than you've learned on TV, in magazines, or from your friends and parents. As a young woman today, it may be challenging to come to terms with your own sexuality. Our culture does not have clearly defined rules about sex, and the messages we get can be really confusing. It's up to us to make sense out of it all.

Your sexuality isn't born when you decide to have sex with someone. Your sexuality belongs to you now. Romance, passion, and sensuality are powerful parts of womanhood. In this chapter, you will hear women and girls talk candidly about everything from first kisses to losing their virginity. They share ways in which their sexuality is part of their whole selves…part of their personalities, their physical selves, and their spirituality.

This is not a reference book on sexuality! We don't expect you to find clear answers in the following pages, but we hope that these stories will stretch your understanding of sexuality and help you begin to ask good questions. One of the secrets to a healthy and rewarding sense of sexuality is getting the information you need. Maybe this chapter can be a place to start.

Something's Changing

Something is different inside of me, and it doesn't have anything to do with my growing breasts, getting pubic hair, or the fact that I got my period last summer. I learned about that stuff in health class and from my mom. This is different.

It's like I feel more now. I know it sounds weird, but I get more excited about things, I worry more than I used to, and my imagination goes crazy sometimes. I have fantasies about everything from kissing guys to running away from home. I think about sex, and I daydream about having babies. I mean, actually having babies. Like, what will it feel like to give birth?

I have a wicked crush on my soccer coach. He's a college guy and he's gorgeous and I think about him all the time. Actually, I think about boys a lot, and wonder if any boys like me. I spend a ton of time getting ready in the morning, and I am always late for the bus. I look at myself in the mirror a lot. It's strange, because last spring I never really cared what I looked like. Now I do.

Part of me wishes these feelings would go away. It was easier when my mind didn't race around so much. But it is pretty exciting. Maybe it is my sexuality coming out. Something's changing!

~ ANONYMOUS, 16

I Wonder

When I look at a tiny little baby, I wonder about the time when I have one of my own. What will it be like to have a baby? I can't imagine pushing a life into the world.

But, even weirder... I wonder what will it be like to make one in the first place? Oh, I know all of that stuff they taught us in school...the parts of the body and how they do this and do that. But the thought of a penis anywhere near my vagina makes me shiver. How could my parents have ever done that? I wonder if they still do it....

I wonder when my feelings about sex will change. It seems so strange to me now. I am starting to look at guys differently, and think about kissing a lot. I hope that by the time I have to make a decision about sex, I will feel ready. I wonder when that will be....

~ MIKKO, 12

The next two stories were written by women who recall the time when they began to notice their budding sexuality.

The Rope Swing

Jill and I never play with dolls any more. Jill likes to play with the boys. She has that same bad way about her that Bobby and Scott have. Jill wishes she were a boy.

Scott has a rope swing, and I rush through my dinner because I know they'll all be there...Scott, and Bobby, and maybe Will. Maybe there will be some girls there, too. I am wearing a halter top that is a little too small now, and my brown legs are scratched and covered with mosquito bites.

My parents are completely taken with me. I know this, and use it to get my way. Right now I want to be excused from dinner so I can play at Scott's rope swing. I know that they'll say yes, as I shovel in the peas. They've made a show of making me finish them, but they smile and say, "All right, go ahead and play, dear." My childlike excitement is valued more than the peas, so I pour it on.

I slide like an otter into the cool thrill of after-dinner freedom. The neighborhood sinks into my skin. I have taken it on as an extension of my house. It all, of course, belongs to me. I can feel the rough warm pavement under my bare feet. I know that when I pass Will's house and make that turn around the bend, the sidewalk slabs will be smoother. I know where the acorns will be thick, and where I will need to cross to the other side of the street because they will hurt my feet. And then I will walk over a wide lawn shadowed by long rays of August sun to the gash in the hill behind Scott's backyard.

There, in the darkening light of the ravine, will hang the rope swing, heavy and pungent with the ripe odor of sweaty hands. Boys' hands.

I have started playing down here at Scott's only just this summer. Jill is the first to bring me to this end of the street. One day, Bobby and Scott take us up to "The Fort," a clubhouse above Scott's garage that is stocked with comic books and Playboy magazines. They let me in only because I am with Jill. They call me by my last name...exploding now and then in bursts of loud laughter that make me flinch, but at the same time fascinate me. Suddenly, without any warning, Bobby pulls down his pants. He shows us all his "wiener," hard and knobby like a hairless little mole.

"Go ahead, touch it," says Jill, smiling like it might as well be hers. So I touch it. Cold and wiggly, it feels like nothing I've ever felt before. I'm confused by all of this, and I giggle nervously as I watch him zip up his pants again. This is new territory...far away from my doll's tea set, my newborn kittens, and my pink bedroom.

The rope swing is in full use at the moment. Jill is showing Martha how to get Bobby off of it by shoving her hand in his crotch. There is a lot of laughter about this. Martha is an "almost babe," meaning she's on the verge of having whatever it is her older sisters have... the stuff that draws boys to them. I am still a "goody-goody." No one knows what I am on the verge of.

I am mostly ignored by the boys, which doesn't bother me too much, yet. At twelve years old, I am still in an "in-between place." I know that my lace curtains will flutter gently at my windows at night. I know I like to play with dolls, even though sometimes I don't want anyone to see me do it. I know I like to sing rhymes and songs, loud and long, as I play on the swing set in my own backyard. But when Bobby gooses me and hands me the rope, whooping out some idiot laugh, finally giving me the turn I've been too shy to ask for, I can't say a thing. For the first time in my life, a boy, this boy, is showing off for my benefit, and I have no voice whatsoever.

I wrap my legs warmly around the fat, hard knot on the end of the rope, and let the red earth flush past below me. I fly out long and slow over the steep ravine. When I swing back, Bobby catches the bottom of the rope to steady me. He puts his hand on my back to help me get off, looks me straight in the eye, and with half a smile whispers quietly in my ear, "You okay?" His kindness surprises me, almost as much as the thick heat I feel within my body. I scramble back up the hill to a safe spot to watch. I am, at this present moment, content just to watch, knowing however, somewhere in my gut, that it may not always be so. No, deep in my body, I know for sure that it will not always be so.

~ DEB, 42, REMEMBERING 12

A Woman Is...

When I was about thirteen, interesting things started to happen to me. My skin seemed to tingle more than usual, and the sun felt stronger on the back of my neck. Sometimes a ripple of warmth ran up my back and down my navel, calling attention to the space between my legs. I became moody and drifted off into sensual dreams. Sometimes I didn't hear people talking to me.

I began to pay more attention to the married couples in the neighborhood. When the adults spoke, I stood quietly by, eavesdropping in hopes of getting a little more information about what it meant to be "a woman." Among themselves, the adults spoke of sexuality in humorous tones, cracking jokes and telling secrets about each other's lives. It was a different story when it came to me. My body hair and bouncing breasts created a worrisome response from the adults in the community. At thirteen, I was no longer the "cute little black girl in petticoats." Now men looked at me and lowered their eyes. The women shook their heads in disgust. For many years, people talked at me, but nobody talked to me. Consequently, I got into a lot of trouble trying to figure out what it meant to be a woman.

This is what I have learned...look for women you feel comfortable talking with about what it means to be a female. Take charge of finding the answers you need, even if the adults in your life at the present time are not open to discussing issues like sexuality. Look for programs, resources, and communities where you can be yourself and get the answers you're looking for.

~ LUISAH, SPIRIT WOMAN,
HALF A CENTURY ON THE EARTH

You are the expert on your own sexuality. When you think of sex, what comes to mind? Here are some thoughts from the girls we have met while writing this book....

When I think of sex, I think of...

"Bonding with another person." –age 17

"Fantasies. Ahhhh!" –age 15

"Close skin." –age 16

"Hard decisions." –age 9

"Being intimate with the one I love." –age 12

"I hope it doesn't hurt too much." –age 15

"Something I am just learning about." –age 10

"Touching, hugging, exploring." –age 14

"Fun." –age 17

"Appreciating and loving one's self." –age 20

"Slimy, sexy, hot." –age 17

"Heavy breathing." –age 18

"I don't know." –age 12

"Two people kissing in a bed." –age 13

"Feeling scared." –age 11

"Naked bodies, touching." –age 11

"Candles, kissing, taking off my clothes." –age 14

"I can't believe that I will actually do that someday!"
    –age 9

When we ask women what comes up when they think about sex, we get a huge variety of answers. Many women talk about their own personal physical sensations and feelings. For them, their sexuality grows out of the fertile ground of their sensuality....

Sensuality

Exploring sensuality is a great way to get to know what is going on inside you and what gives you pleasure. You can expand your sensuality by exploring each of the five senses in ways like these:

Touch. Rub a smooth stone on your skin. Stroke yourself with a feather. Walk out in the rain without a coat. Your skin is your greatest sense organ. Listen to it. Notice what fabrics feel great on your body, and wear them.

Sight. Gaze deeply into a starry night. Watch a fuzzy caterpillar crawling on the sidewalk. When you read magazines or look at art, what color combinations attract you? What colors soothe you? Make you feel great? Those are your healing colors. Wear colors that fit your mood.

Smell. Walk in the woods and take in the scents. What are the heavenly aromas in your kitchen at home? What perfumes attract you at the department store? Notice the scents of other people.

Taste. Really notice the flavor splash of the first chomp on a piece of bubble gum. What foods do you love? Eat a meal in slow motion. Can you taste twice as much by eating half as fast?

Sound. Just like seeing as far as your eye can see, practice hearing as far as your ear can hear. Listen to every sound in a moment. What music delights you? Makes you sad? Calms you? Listen to the fullness of silence.

Above all, learn what causes you to feel alive and sensual in your body. Develop a "menu" of favorite sights, sounds, touches, and tastes, and indulge in them often, as long as they are not hazardous to your health!

Sensuality is the younger sister of sexuality. When you get to know her first, she'll blossom into the lovely sister of sexuality.

~ ANONYMOUS, 36

This is one woman's description of how she experiences her own sexuality…

A Gift to Myself

When I think of sex, I imagine languid long legs, skin against skin. Steaming showers, the smell of lavender, and tensions released…playfully exploring, recognizing sensations, and discovering new ones…a dance of giving and receiving, being present in the moment, allowing myself to feel, be held, be loved…a gift to myself. Thoughts drift away and I enter a space more deeply connected to who I am.

I feel suspended by golden silken threads. My chest shivers. The best moments occur when I allow myself to simply focus on my body's sensations. As I give and receive, I notice textures, skin, muscles, firmness, softness, contours of bone and flesh, hair, folds, and curves.

When I think of sex, I am in awe of all that we are…the sensitivity of a fingertip's touch, the tickle of lips grazing my face, and whispers in my ear…. I am carried. I am held. Giving away and giving to myself.

~ ANONYMOUS, 42

Young women are sometimes curious about how sex really feels. This woman shares her reflections on the experience of orgasm.

ORGASM

When I was seven,
I felt the first whispers of sexual pleasure.
I remember that certain way that I could lay across the piano
    bench,
Or sit sideways on the handmade wooden swing in our backyard,
Or rock gently on the pillows that overflowed on my bed.
I didn't understand what that feeling was, or why it happened,
    but it was wonderful....
It felt moist, warm, rhythmic.

When I was ten,
I remember hearing my friends talk about exploring their private
    parts,
With their fingers, with handles of hairbrushes, with anything
    that "fit."
I acted disgusted.
But, secretly, alone in my dark room at night, I did it too.
It felt moist, warm, rhythmic.

When I was seventeen,
I made love to a man for the first time.
I was ready and felt that I made the right decision.
It was exciting, tender, and romantic,

But it wasn't what I expected...
It felt moist, warm, rhythmic.

Then, when I was twenty-seven,
After many years of learning to intimately know
Myself, my body, and my partner...
I felt the most expanding, mind-blowing experience of my life.
From some primal place, deep inside of me,
From the place where
Moist, warm rhythms had sent out their prophecies for two
   decades,
My first orgasm burst through me.
Ancient waves of deep, earthy pleasure,
Pulling me out of myself and in to myself at the same time.
Joyful, and full of energy and life, I remember thinking,
"So, this is what all the excitement is about."

Now I know that orgasm is just one expression of sexual pleasure
And it "comes" in many different packages.
Different at different times in our lives,
Different for different women,
Different every time.

   ~anonymous, 33

Some of us remember the moment when we felt our first waves of sexual attraction...a first kiss, a slow dance, or our first real crush. As a teenager, your first experiences with romance and exploring your sexuality can be exciting, but confusing too.

Macarena or Slow Dance?

Dear Diary,

Am I the only girl who hasn't been asked to dance by a boy? Dances are a big deal at my school. Friday nights, once a month, our school has a dance, and my friends and I dance all night long. We do the Macarena, we go wild to the "YMCA" song, and we all learned how to do the Electric Slide. But now, some of the girls my age have been asked to slow dance with boys. Not me.

Some girls have slow danced with so many guys that I wonder if they do it to keep score. It gives them something to brag about in school on Monday. I do have some friends who haven't slow danced yet, so we are in the same boat. My friend Charlotte danced with a boy last Friday. He's the shyest, quietest boy in school. No one else would dance with him, but Charlotte said it was actually fun. When will it be my turn?

one month later...

Dear Diary,

Yes! A boy finally asked me to dance with him. His name is Kevin and he's really nice. I like him and I think he likes me too. He is the first guy I've ever danced with, besides with my Dad in the kitchen. I was so nervous! But once we started to dance together, it was really fun. Slow dancing with Kevin was really cool. I wouldn't have traded those two hours at the dance for anything!

Now I have another problem. Two of my closest friends haven't slow danced yet, and I feel funny that I am so excited about dancing with Kevin. Jess says she's not ready to dance with a boy, but Helena would give anything to dance with Colin. They tease me a little about liking Kevin, but it's mostly joking.

I wouldn't "go out" with Kevin, because I'm not even sure what that means anyway. It's just fun hanging out with boys my age. It's not a crime or anything, but it does feel a little different. Sometimes it's even more fun being with Kevin than with my girlfriends. That's okay too, isn't it?

~ LEAH, 12

With the exception of situations of sexual harassment or sexual abuse, we all have choices about when and with whom we begin to explore our sexuality. As teenagers, sometimes unsure about who we really are, it is easy to forget that we can speak up for ourselves when we are in a physically intimate situation. Our desire to feel attractive, accepted, and loved can cloud our feelings about what we really want to happen.

This woman looks back at her first sexually intimate experience and wishes that she had made a different choice. She learned through her experience. Now she shares her wisdom with you.

The Lion's Roar

I will never forget the roar of the lion. How cruel it was of that old man up the road to keep the lion caged in his backyard. At night I could hear his freedom cry, and although I never actually visited him, his song of longing reminded me that he was real.

I often questioned what was real in my family: the safe, daytime image of perfection, or the scary nights when alcoholism turned things upside-down. I felt a kinship with the lion. I longed for freedom, too.

Although I was only thirteen, I went out with kids who were much older than I was. One midsummer night, I was invited to go to a boy/girl camp-out with a guy I had been seeing for a couple of weeks. Knowing that my parents would never allow me to go, I decided to sneak out of the house.

Urged on by the roar of the lion, I slipped quietly out my bedroom window and crept alone, through the dark, to my friend's backyard. In the shadows, my boyfriend met me there and led me to the tents, where a number of couples were necking and making out. Feeling both scared and excited to be free, I followed my boyfriend into a green canvas army tent.

That night, although I was never forced to do anything against my will, part of my thirteen-year-old self was emotionally bruised. As I lay there, my boyfriend touched parts of my body that I had not yet explored myself. Without even realizing what was happening, I gave away part of my sexuality before I had even claimed it as my own. I was left feeling empty and unable to talk to anyone about my confusion. I didn't sense that any of the other girls who came out of those tents that night felt the way I did.

I walked home alone. As I climbed back through my window, I heard the lion's lonely song again. Perhaps he knew. My escape had not brought me freedom, only another cage that I would have to climb out of some day.

As I look back, I wish that someone in my life had taught me about the power and beauty of my own sexuality. I was never invited to acknowledge myself as a sexual being, let alone shown options about how to explore and express myself in that way. Now I am thankful that my sexuality and sensuality find voices through music, dancing, nature, art, food, romance, friendships, and an exciting sexual relationship with my partner of twenty-two years.

As you become a woman, remember that your sexuality belongs to you, not someone else. Search for a way to make it your own before you decide to share it!

~ ANONYMOUS, 39

How to Say "NO!"

If you have a boyfriend, and he is the greatest thing in your life, fantastic! But don't mess it up by falling into bed or the back seat of a car too soon. Use your tongue! That means talk about it. Decide what feels right for you, and then talk about it together. Don't give your partner mixed signals. Try not to play games. Agree from the beginning how far you want to go, and don't change your mind in the middle of everything. Stay strong and conscious.

And a word or two about those famous sex lines:

"If you really loved me you would..."

Maybe if he really loved you, he wouldn't ask you to do something that you are not ready to do. If he is willing to leave you over this issue, he may not be someone who will stand by you when you really need help and support.

"You're killing me! You get me all excited and then turn it off! What do you expect me to do?"

Don't let him put a guilt trip on you. He is in charge of his feelings and his body, not you. If he really is sexually frustrated and needs a release, suggest that he masturbate. People do it all the time, and it can be a really healthy alternative to having sex before you are ready.

"Having sex won't change anything."

Oh, yes it will. Having sex with someone changes things a lot! Sometimes for the better, and sometimes not. And you can't always tell which way it's going to go. If you really value your relationship, go slow. Enjoy the romance!

~ ANDREA, 30,
TEACHER FROM SWITZERLAND

One of the biggest decisions we face as we become mature women is when and with whom to have sex. This decision is incredibly complex. In one ear we hear the media making sex sound fun and exciting, and in the other we learn of the fatal risks of AIDS and the danger of sexually transmitted diseases.

The following stories are from girls who each have a different perspective on the decision to become sexually active. The common advice in their stories seems to be this: Make conscious, educated choices that are in line with your own values and that protect your physical and emotional health.

Losing Virginity

It was the cast party. I was smoking clove cigarettes on the porch swing when he showed up. He sat down beside me and we talked about school. The party went on and we danced, watched the video of the play, and ended up going upstairs by ourselves. My heart raced as I pretended to be the sophisticated one. When he kissed me, it sent chills up my spine. As we pulled away from each other, we exchanged a look that told me what was about to happen. I pulled his T-shirt and sweater over his head. He kissed my lips, my neck, my breasts. I stood and took off my stockings. I turned out the lights. We threw the rest of our clothes into the darkness. We made out, and felt each other's skin in a feeble attempt at foreplay. Then he was on top of me. It happened so fast. Before I knew it, we were having sex.

I felt happy, but don't get me wrong…there were no fireworks or sudden feelings of utmost maturity. I was too relieved that the whole ordeal didn't hurt and that I wasn't bleeding all over the new futon to pay attention to pleasure, if there was any. It was over in about twenty minutes. His friend knocked on the door to say it was time to go. We scrambled to find our clothing. He kissed me good-bye, said he would call, and left.

Then the pain began. All I wanted to do was cry. I had gotten my wish. I was now "officially a woman." But all I could think about was what a messy rite of passage it was.

It doesn't have to be like this.

~ ANONYMOUS, 16

Experience Isn't Always the Best Teacher

I am not a virgin, but for a long time I have wished I could turn back the clock and reclaim my virginity. I thought that by sleeping with guys I would learn how to be a good lover. Now I realize how wrong I was.

For the first time in my life, I am in a serious relationship with a man. I have learned more about love and lovemaking in the past year than in all of my previous experiences combined. The most important lesson for me is that true intimacy and sexual pleasure come with honesty and commitment, not multiple experiences.

~ KERI, 20

Not Front Page News

Sex was always a hot topic of conversation in my high school, so even though I wasn't having sex, I didn't want people to know I was a virgin. I thought that boys would think I was weird or something. When the topic came up, I would either lie or change the subject.

When I went away to college, something changed. My friends at school knew I was a virgin. In fact, half of them were virgins also! Suddenly, it didn't bother me that people knew the same information that I had tried so hard to keep secret.

~ ANONYMOUS, 21

So what do you do with all of that passion and excitement that bubbles up when you begin to mature sexually? Enjoy it! But that doesn't necessarily mean acting on it. Sometimes....

"The best part about sex is wanting it."

When I first heard that phrase, it made no sense. After all, I learned that sex was something you "had" or something you "got." The gossip around school was all about who had had sex, not about who wanted it. Secretly, we all wanted it! Many years later, I think I finally understand what that phrase means.

Sexual desire is a power beyond words. It is a hunger that is sometimes too quickly fed. In a culture that encourages a "quick fix," desire is not often experienced to its fullest. The wanting, the longing, can be felt in many delicious ways...in the rush of blood that surges to your cheeks when the guy you like walks around the corner at school...in the electric current that runs through your body in the dangling moment just before a first kiss...in the bittersweet ache that you feel when you are separated from the one that you love...in the juicy, romantic anticipation of a candlelit dinner...in the slippery slow motion unbuttoning of your shirt for your lover...and within the magical suspended moment just before you experience an orgasm.

When you recognize the gift of desire, you can begin to see the wisdom in the phrase, "The best part about sex is wanting it." You can enjoy being sexy, sensual, and aroused, without necessarily "having" sex. Believe it or not, many of us who have been sexually active still think that a huge part of the excitement about sex is in the desire itself...in just wanting it! Those tingly lusty waves you feel are precious. Enjoy them while you can, because when a sexual urge or need is met, desire fades. This is not to say that excitement and desire can't be nurtured and preserved in a long-term, loving relationship. It can. But now is a beautiful time to learn to honor your desires. Savor your luscious longings patiently. Take time to learn from them. They are wise teachers.

~ ANONYMOUS, 47

Each and every one of us has a unique way of experiencing and expressing our sexuality. The following stories were written by girls and women who have recognized themselves as lesbians or bisexuals. Our society has come a long way in accepting a variety of sexual orientations, but adolescent girls who identify themselves as non-heterosexual can still have a difficult time feeling comfortable with their sexuality....

The Biggest Crush

The biggest crush that I ever had was on Sandee. She was a senior when I was a sophomore in college. She was the most talented actor in school, and she was wild, irresponsible, and beautiful. Not beautiful like a model, but big and curvy, with skin the color of coffee with cream. She was wacky and funny, and she thought I was cool. As far as I knew, Sandee was straight and so was I. I dated guys and thought that she did, too. Even so, I would sweat a little when she paid attention to me in front of my friends.

Sandee got me a job where she worked, and I was in heaven! Sometimes after work, we would grab some dinner and go for a walk. One day it rained, but we walked anyway. It was then that I realized that what I felt for Sandee was more than a crush. I really loved her. The strangest part was that I had a feeling that she felt something for me, too.

The following week we were at a party, and she began flirting with me. I flirted back. I felt powerful and beautiful and scared. What did this mean? After the party, we walked back to her apartment and she kissed me. Wow! I had kissed guys. I had lost my virginity some time before. But, wow! This feeling was new, and I really liked it. I went home and I couldn't sleep.

That summer with Sandee was when I experienced my first sexual relationship with a woman. It felt lovely, yet dangerous. It was natural and right and good.

Sandee left at the end of the summer, and we stayed in touch for a while. I often think of that walk in the rain and the incredible feelings she freed in me that summer, and I smile.

~ HEATHER, 28

I THINK I AM IN LOVE

I am in love I think,

With the bone beneath the neck that

Protrudes ever so slightly.

In love with the nose, the perfectly laid fingers, and with the

Soft voice that speaks only what needs to be said.

But I am also alone. Alone in myself.

I cannot tell anyone. I cannot gossip with my friends, cannot
    giggle,

As the nose, the neck, the soft voice walks by.

Instead I turn my head and hide.

Is it because the fingers are long and thin,

The voice high and melodic, and the skin soft and feminine?

I am not ashamed, not unhappy with myself,

Just alone with untold love.

It hurts something awful sometimes to even look at her

Without wincing in pain.

But in the end I am still in love.

Alone, aching, but still wonderfully in love

with the nose, the fingers, the voice,

and with her.

~anonymous, 16

The last few stories in this chapter are simply love stories. Each one reflects the ecstatic, confusing, bittersweet feelings of falling in love.

Encounters with a Frog Prince

I remember first noticing him out in front of school. We were gathered in circles, milling about, waiting for the bell to ring. He was on his skateboard whirling around, doing ollies. He was wearing navy blue and gray flannel pants, an icy blue T-shirt, Converse sneakers, and a Detroit Tigers baseball cap. His jet black hair poked out ever so slightly in back. When he removed his hat, to my delight, his chin-length bangs spilled forward, covering one eye. In all of my twelve years, I had never seen such a hunk of burning love. And he did not even know that I was alive. Not yet, anyway. Jeremiah would be mine. Oh, yeah, mine!

Apparently a lot of girls felt the same way that I did, because every couple of weeks Jeremiah had a new girlfriend. He was always the one to end the relationship...a ladies' man. I swooned as he dated all of my friends, and when he dyed those gorgeous bangs blonde and pierced his ear, I thought he couldn't become any more beautiful.

On my first day of science in eighth grade, I plunked myself down at a desk and scanned the room. There sat Jeremiah Myers just two seats behind me! If I leaned my chair way back and stretched really far, I could touch him. The teacher's voice drew me back to the front of the room. She was putting people into pairs to do an introductory exercise. "Katie and Jeremiah, do you know each other?" she asked. We nodded our heads. "Good! You are a pair."

Jeremiah and I, a pair! It was melodious to my ears. Honestly, I think that Mrs. McSweeny regretted ever putting us together. Every day the two of us would slip into our desk built for two and laugh and gossip during the whole class. Forget the Mesozoic and Cenozoic eras! The present moment was much more important to me.

One glorious day, he asked for my phone number. My hands trembled as I wrote down the seven digits. I wiped my sweating palms on my Umbros, adjusted my ponytail, and gave him the number.

That night I paced back and forth. My stomach gurgled as I awaited his call. Minutes passed. Hours passed. Finally, after my third bowl of mint chocolate chip ice cream, the phone rang. I ran for it, snatching it out of the clutches of my younger sister. It wasn't him. It was my friend, Kate. "Did he call you yet?" she asked. I began to moan about it, only to be interrupted by call waiting. I took a deep breath and told her to hold on. I never did click back over. It was Jeremiah. We made small talk for a while. Okay, until well after my bedtime. I crawled up into my bunk bed and cradled the phone under the covers. Hours later, I heard my mom's footsteps coming closer. "Jeremiah, I have to go. My mom will kill me if she knows I'm still on the phone." "Wait." he said. "There's something I have to ask you. Will you, um, go out with me?" Though I was bursting with joy, I kept my cool. I heard somewhere that it's not good to show too much excitement with a guy. "Sure, I guess," I said, five Mississippi's later.

Our relationship was a simple one. He would write me beautiful letters. He couldn't spell for shit, but whatever he lacked in spelling ability, he made up for in poetics and sweetness. He told me how pretty I was, and how glad he was that we were going out (even long after his usual two-week limit for girlfriends had expired). We never saw each other outside of school, until he wrote me a note asking if "maybe" I wanted to go to Derek's Valentine's Day party with him.

A week later, my mom dropped me off in front of Derek's house. I made my way into the house and wove through the crowd to Jeremiah. He smiled and grabbed my hand as we joined the ranks of couples moving two by two, like animals on their way to Noah's Ark. We all went downstairs to the family room. Some people played pool…some talked. Then someone turned out the lights.

Jeremiah pulled me so close that I could smell him. We stood there in the dark, surrounded by bunches of other couples, dancing to a silent song. I felt his cheek against mine. Then he pulled away slightly. I could make out the silhouette of his face moving closer and closer until I felt his lips press against mine. That night, before I had left for the party, I'd written a diary entry of the future, just to assure that this moment would occur. It read: "Tonight for the first time I kissed a boy, and better yet, it was Jeremiah." It really happened.

After that night, Jeremiah was totally into me. His calling increased, and so did his letters. I remember receiving one letter, specially folded up. On the cover he had written:

JEREMIAH + KATIE

You would think that I would be pretty ecstatic about all of this, right? Well actually, I felt pretty damn crowded. A few weeks later, I broke up with Jeremiah, in a note, of course. I'm not sure what I was thinking, because I still liked him.

I wish I could tell you why I did that to him (and Brian, and Kevin, and Steve, and Ben, and Dennis...), but I can't. On more than one occasion, after I have broken up with someone, I've been asked, "Why are you crying so hard? It's over. It's what you wanted." It's just not that simple.

I am, unfortunately, a "grass is always greener on the other side of the fence" kind of girl. My yo-yo, "come here, go away" emotions have caused many people bushels of hurt. I am working on it.

As far as Jeremiah goes, I believe that it's a good thing that we broke up. Okay, so we did get back together a couple more times. It just didn't work out, though. I am really glad to say that we've always remained friends.

One interesting pattern that I've noticed as I've looked back is that whenever Jeremiah and I would start dating, he would just happen to shave some body part. The first time it was those beautiful bangs that I was so wild about, then his eyebrows, and then his legs. I really think it's for the best that we stopped dating when we did. I don't wanna even think about what he would've shaved off next....

~ KATHRYN, 20

First Love

In the honey sweat of summer, I listened for the sound of his breath. Steve. My first love. As he inhaled, I could see the sharp points of his ribcage begin to take form. They poked against the pale, skim-milk blue of his T-shirt as we sat beneath the stars at the pond behind the school. The ducks made sleep sounds in the peaceful night air. In the innocence of youth, our only touch was the soft fingerprint of words that brushed across the space between us. We spoke in sacred whispers of the dreams of young romantics who were stuck in suburbia, of our loss of faith in our parents and preachers, and of the immense relief in having found each other within the loneliness of growing up. Beneath the sound of his voice, enclosed in the shadow of his skinny shoulders, I was small and green, dipping my toes into the water, careful not to get wet.

By the time June came, the fever was already taking hold of me. I could not stop myself from spending every second with him. We would lie on his bed while Frank Sinatra records from the downtown thrift store crackled on the stereo. We would go for midnight walks, and he'd pull me into the middle of the street to dance under the lights that filtered down through the windows of nearby houses. Even when he wasn't with me, he was there.

An hour after we parted each night, the feel of his breath was still warm and damp in my lungs. I would sit on the porch, the fabric of my cotton nightgown sticking to my skin, taking in the lemon drop candy smell that I had already begun to recognize as my own, and humming the bars to the song he wrote on his guitar. I could spend the whole night like that, just thinking about him with my shoulders pushed back and my head held high.

Maybe that should have been my first warning. After about three months of humming his songs, spending every waking hour with him, getting closer to finding the core of his soul, I had a frightening revelation. My parents were watching some horrible sitcom on television downstairs. The sound of the canned laughter reached my ears in the bathroom while I was getting ready to go out with him. I half-listened to the exchange of dialogue. Through the strange acoustics around the shower door, I could hear a young boy ask his mother how he would know if he were in love. Just as I picked up my things to leave, I caught her response. "You know you love someone when you care more about them than you care about yourself." Suddenly I felt sick. I quickly shot a glance at my reflection in the mirror. It was exactly what I had been afraid of. My face was the same, but my eyes looked strange. I thought, "My God, I am in love with this boy."

This is not the way it was supposed to happen! When I felt it for the first time, it was supposed to be discovered in an epiphany during a lonely night on a journey far away from home. Or when he suddenly uttered those three little words in the perfect stillness by the pond. But instead, it had found me through the cliché that some no-name writer had probably thrown together on a bus ride to Hollywood. I was repulsed. I was scared. I was in love. To an independent young woman, this was the most frightening thought in the world.

I had to hold on to the banister as I walked down the stairs. I made it down to the bottom step and said good-bye to my parents. But as soon as I closed the door behind me, everything changed. I couldn't go back. Everything was different now.

Before I knew it, my best friend was calling me, crying on the phone because I never wanted to go out with her anymore. My parents were calling every hospital in town when I came home at 2:00 A.M., three hours after my curfew. I was waiting outside on the porch, writing bad poems on the backs of paper plates, waiting, waiting for him to drop by. He would always show up just as I was giving up to go back inside.

In the dark on the front porch one night, he became serious. "I have something to tell you," he said. Slowly, he opened his hands for me, revealing his silver pocket watch. We sat there for hours in the absolute stillness, just listening to the sound of the watch ticking. The contorted figures of my parents were large and deep blue through the yellow windows upstairs. Beneath them he was bathed in a soft light, one silent finger to his lips, the image of complete calm. And suddenly I knew. He didn't have to say a word. I knew what was coming next.

September 7th. I still remember the date. The last night before he moved away...3,500 miles away. The whole night we were just biding our time. We didn't know what to do. After all of this time and intimacy, we had regressed back to the status of our first date. We walked out to his car more slowly than I thought was humanly possible. And he kissed me good-bye there, beneath the balcony of my parents' room, angled against the garage door so they couldn't see me in the shadow. I could taste the salt from my own tears on his lips.

It was all I could do to let go of him, to turn around and walk away, slowly, deliberately, one foot in front of the other, my hands opening and closing like the mouths of tiny fish on land. I thought that if I could just make it to the door without looking back, then I could make it through the coming months without him. But I couldn't. I looked back. I caught his expression one last time as he stood there behind his car with his arms and chin resting on the roof. I already knew something had changed. I closed my eyes and whispered, "It's dead."

And the reason why I couldn't stop crying, the real reason, wasn't just that love was lost. My childhood was over.

~ MELISSA, 18

That Cute Guy

I had a golden childhood. My life was smooth. I had a lot of good friends and a nice family. I was known as "sweet, but gullible." I got teased a lot.

In junior high, things started to change. School became challenging. I began to menstruate, and my emotions were like a wild ride on a roller coaster. One morning in seventh grade, I fell in love with a cute guy who showed up in class. We girls thought he was "a doll." He seemed to love the attention he was getting from all of us, but before long, he began to pay attention to me in particular.

That summer, I decided to go to camp with my friends. The "cute guy" was there also, and I was in heaven. I met a bunch of new friends, and even had a built-in boyfriend! By Wednesday of the first week, it all changed. His early adolescent eye started roaming, and by the end of the week, we were no longer a couple. The summer was ruined!

On our very first day back at school in the fall, he leaned against my locker and suggested that we start going together again. I was relieved, said "okay," and we were a couple the rest of the year.

The same scenario happened the summer after eighth grade. And the first day of school, he once again asked me to be his girl. This time I said something like, "No way, you jerk!" and walked away.

For the first time in my life, I felt great personal strength. It was as though I had discovered a totally different part of myself. He continued to pursue me, but for a year and a half I delighted in my sense of personal power. The sense of strength and honoring myself that I learned during that time has always stuck with me. It is so easy for a girl to forget, or not even know, the strength of her own personhood when it comes to her budding sexuality.

All of this took place fifty years ago, and I am still married to that cute guy who walked into my seventh-grade classroom!

~ JOAN, 61, TEACHER, COMPOSER

And one last great thing to think about....

Falling In Love

Here it is…the secret to romance, great sex and long term commitment: *Fall in love…with yourself!*

Fall in love with *you* before you get involved with someone else. Learn what you love. Be romantic. Be creative. Express yourself. Explore your sensuality. Learn what gives you sexual pleasure, *alone!* Play. Be curious. Love yourself by experiencing all of who you are. Be comfortable with being alone. You are whole and beautiful when you are alone. Go ahead and fall madly in love…with yourself. If you do, someday when Cupid's arrow hits you, you'll survive, even if your heart gets a little bruised!

~ JOANNAH, 41

How Can I Handle One More Thing?

Crisis in Adolescence

hen a crisis occurs during your adolescent years, it may feel especially overwhelming. Like most girls, you're wondering about making good choices, speaking up for yourself, fitting in with friends, taking care of your body as it changes. Suddenly there is much more to deal with than "the usual stuff"...maybe a personal problem you are facing alone, or a crisis in your family, in your neighborhood, in school, or somewhere out in the world.

The experiences that girls and women have shared on the pages ahead sound like a laundry list of the world's worst nightmares...accidents, illnesses, divorce, rape, loss, addictions, war. Unfortunately, life is not always pleasant, and crises can occur during adolescence as easily as during any other time in life. But if you read between the lines in the stories shared, you will notice that even through crises, important lessons can be learned. You can make it through a painful situation, gaining wisdom and growing stronger along the way.

I am a scared little girl with no place to hide.

I wonder what the world would be like without fear or violence.

I hear the trees crying out as they fall to the ground.

I see a kidnapper grabbing me when I am in the woods.

I want there to be no fear in this world.

I am a scared little girl with no place to hide.

I pretend I don't know that anything bad is happening.

I feel the pain in the stomachs of all the starving children.

I touch the wounds of a dying soldier.

I worry that I won't be able to do anything with my life.

I cry for all those who need someone to cry with them.

I am a scared little girl with no place to hide.

I understand that not everything in the world is bad.

I dream of a perfect life.

I say we need to think more of others than we do of ourselves.

I try as hard as I can to see the good side of everything.

I hope for more smiles than tears.

But I am still a scared little girl with no place to hide.

~Megan, 14

Upside-down at Seventeen

I was a senior in high school. I had been driving tractors and farm trucks since I was twelve, so my parents had no problem letting me use their pick-up truck to go to a school event that Saturday morning. My friend Laurel was with me.

After the fun at school was over, our hearts singing from the time we had spent with our classmates, we headed west towards home. Dark, gloomy clouds suddenly burst open, and a heavy rain fell around us as we drove along in the old truck. The windshield wipers were dancing as fast as they could, and I decided to slow down. Suddenly things seemed out of control. I was trying to keep the truck away from the muddy shoulder. We slid across the blacktop. The next thing I remember, we were upside-down in the truck, next to an apple tree in the orchard.

How could such joy suddenly turn to such terror? Neither of us was hurt; not even a scratch! A true miracle since the truck was now kissing the trunk of an apple tree. We were immediately surrounded by people peering inside the truck. They helped us get out, and my mind started working again. What was I going to do now? How was I going to get the truck upright before my father saw it? Daddy! Oh, my gosh! What would he do?

I didn't have long to think about this, because soon I saw those eyes in the crowd, those familiar eyes that could always discipline me with no words necessary. The crowd helped turn the truck back over, and it was then that Daddy spoke. "Get in that truck and take Laurel home." "No!" I replied. "I don't ever want to drive again!" My father repeated himself, insisting that I drive Laurel home right away.

It was the best thing he could have done for me. I drove my friend home, then went home myself. The incident was never mentioned again by my father, and my driving privileges were not limited in any way. I'm sure I never would have driven again if he hadn't been so insistent that day.

This memory illustrates the depth of emotions that teenage girls often feel. From such high joys to the depths of despair, all in a split second. The embarrassment of people staring at me and at my mistake; the fear of my father's reaction; the relief when I discovered that my friend and I were okay. Emotions are so close to the surface during these years, and teenagers feel more pain than they need to sometimes.

The world didn't stop because I turned my father's truck upside down, and it won't stop for any of the other disappointments or failures you might have along the way. Face your joys and your sorrows, and you will be "right side up" before you know it!

~ ELMA, 70, MOTHER, GRANDMOTHER, GREAT-GRANDMOTHER

Life gets crazy sometimes. No wonder we all feel overwhelmed! This young woman has found a way to feel better when it all seems like too much to handle....

Stressed Out!

It's all building up inside of me. Stress from school, stress from my friends, stress from my family. I have too many responsibilities, and all I want to do is relax, unwind, and clear my head. I get depressed and lonely when I can't slow it all down.

Different things bring it on, like being separated from my true love for over six months. Or how I want to be a certain kind of person, but I'm always messing up along the way. I think about choices I've made for my life so far, and wonder if I should have taken a different path. I feel stupid and fat, and not good enough for anyone. This huge weight is on my shoulders, and everyone seems to have a better life than I do.

Sometimes I just lie in bed and cry for awhile, which actually helps a lot. I also write everything down in my diary...what happened, how I'm feeling. Then I watch the funniest video I have, and don't always laugh, but I feel better anyway. After that, I take a nap, and if it's late, sleep until morning.

I always feel better when I wake up and read what I wrote in my diary. I think about why I was upset, and replace my bad thoughts with better ones. My mind's eye wakes up and sees the world as it really is, and I remember what is true and right.

I know I'm not crazy for feeling like this, and I know I won't feel down forever. The stress gets me down, but it's part of life. I've learned what works for me when it's time to just let go.

~ ANONYMOUS, 18

Sometimes changes occur in our families that are out of our control. The separation and divorce of parents unfortunately takes place quite often, and our parents' problems suddenly become problems for us, too.

Accepting Divorce...Accepting Me

I have hardly left the depths of being a teenager. The most challenging thing I have faced during my adolescence has not been trying to fit in, or breaking away from my mother, or expressing my "true self." It has been dealing with divorced parents.

I never felt like their divorce was my fault, but the guilt that I have experienced throughout my childhood and early adolescent years has been immense. I remember feeling guilty whenever I did anything slightly wrong, such as leaving a glass on the counter, or leaving lights on in a room when I left. I always felt the need to be perfect so that my father and others around me would accept me.

Now I have trouble accepting myself. I thought I needed to be some-one else; someone better. To this day, I don't feel like my father accepts me or appreciates me for who I am. During the rapid growth of these incred-ible teenage years, this has been one of my biggest obstacles.

However, the love of my mother, stepfather, and friends has given me strength and courage to face what I'm up against. Their love and never-ending support has been very important to me. They have taught me that the darkest part of the day is right before dawn, and that I should never, ever give up. I won't!

~ DEBRA, 14, LOVER OF FLYING COWS

A Family Torn

I will never forget the night we found out that my mother was not returning from her "vacation." Our family was moving again because of my father's job. After months of packing, my mother told us she was going to take a brief vacation, then meet us in our new home. My father, sister, and I went ahead to settle in before the school year began.

After our first week there, we received a postcard from Mom. She wrote that her trip had been delayed because she had gotten the flu, but added that she would be with us again in a week or two. A month passed, and there was still no sign of Mom. In a birthday card for my sister, who was turning eleven, Mom enclosed a letter to Dad. My sister assumed it was for her, read it, then angrily threw it down. She began to yell, "I hate her! She's not my mother anymore!" The note informed my father to take Mom off the insurance plans and other important records. She was not coming back to the family.

I was totally blown away that Mom had decided to leave us! When Dad came home, I handed him the letter. I thought he would die right there in front of my eyes. He just kept repeating, "Oh, God! Oh, God! What am I supposed to do now?" He cried, and my sister was hysterical. I felt I had to be strong. I began to frantically clean the house. It was now going to be up to me to keep this family together. Suddenly I wasn't fifteen anymore. I had crossed over into adulthood in one moment's time. I had to take over as "Mom," and became responsible for many family tasks.

We didn't eat dinner that night. Somehow, dinner was never the same.

~ RUTH, 24,
EARLY CHILDHOOD EDUCATOR

The Peacekeeper

My parents had a troubled marriage. For many years, my father had an affair with another woman, and it caused nightly tension in our household. Mom and Dad argued constantly, leaving my brother and me in the background hearing the family crash down around us. My older sisters were involved in their own way too, and our family life was as troubled as the marriage itself.

Mom finally decided that she wanted the marriage to end, but my father chose to cling to the image of the "family man"...nice house, good job, wife and kids. As Mom pushed to get out of the marriage, Dad insisted that she would never be able to support the children on her own. She stayed, and I spent my adolescence being the peacekeeper in the family, trying desperately to make everything seem okay.

As I look at my own children now, and see their teenage years filled with choices, interests, and activities, I realize that I simply did not live that part of my life. I never made choices about what I wanted to do; I only made choices based on what I thought would make my family or others happy. My creativity could never be expressed, as I was too busy trying to keep the peace. I hope my children will make their own choices, express themselves, and not simply focus on pleasing their father or me.

I lost my true teenage self because of my parents' problems. If your parents' marriage is broken and overflowing with conflict, remember that it's not up to you to repair it.

~ MARY ANN, 41

In many areas of the world today, war is a very real part of life. This woman remembers what it was like for her to leave her childhood behind in a time of war.

Robbed By War

War is a scary thing to deal with, no matter what your age. I was almost thirteen when the announcement came over the radio at my grandparents' house. The United States was now at war. It was December 7th, 1941, the day Pearl Harbor was bombed.

There was nothing to like about World War II. I was mad at Hitler for starting it all. I especially hated that my father had enlisted in the Army and went overseas. I cried and waved good-bye as he boarded the bus at the courthouse square in the center of our small town. He left behind a wife and four children. I was the oldest.

We worried about a lot of things while he was gone. Would America be invaded by enemy troops? We had air raid drills at school to practice protecting ourselves, just in case bombs were dropped here in America. We worried about whether my father would return. Would I ever hear him sing those wonderful old songs again, with his eyes sparkling and his British accent filling the air? Food was rationed, and it was a time filled with hardship. In the midst of all this, my sister and I were soon to be teenagers. The changes that naturally occur with those years only seemed harder when war was always in the back of your mind.

The war eventually ended, and my father did return. Our family was never the same, though. While he was gone, I had to grow up fast, taking care of my family in an adult way at a time when I needed to just be me. I learned that I could be responsible for a lot and do a good job with whatever came my way, but war in the midst of those important teenage years robbed me of more than I care to remember.

~ MARY, 67, MOM AND GRANDMA

Addiction to alcohol and drugs affects more than just the person using and abusing. This teenager tells of her experiences with an alcoholic father, followed by an older woman's story of pain and recovery for her family and her alcoholic mother.

Too Many Bottles

My father drinks a quart of liquor every night. I have smelled it on his breath, but I never really knew how much he drank until I watched him tackle an entire bottle of gin, right before my eyes.

I'm lying in my bedroom trying to go to sleep, and I can hear the sound of ice clinking in his glass as he prepares his next "potion" of gin or vodka. He's in the living room, and he'll probably spend the rest of the night there, drinking and watching television, getting drunker by the hour. When I see him still there in the morning, I want to believe that he just fell asleep, but deep down I know that he has passed out cold.

My mother sits quietly at the dining room table, working on crossword puzzles, reading novels, silently counting the empty liquor bottles in the trash. She would probably like to do fun things with Dad, but his drinking always comes first. The bottles always win out over my brother and me, too. Whenever we ask Dad to play catch with us in the backyard or to help us with our homework, he says no.

I don't know what to do. I tried to talk to Dad about it, but he got mad and told me I was wrong. I saw a poster at school about Alateen meetings, but he'd probably kill me if he ever found out I went to one. I feel so alone. I tried drinking beer at a party once, but I didn't want to get caught. I sure don't want to end up like Dad. I'm never drinking again, no matter what my friends say.

Sometimes I walk around the neighborhood at night, wishing that our family could be like the other families on our block. The bottles always win that one, too. I think I'll find out when the next Alateen meeting is, and go to it, and just listen. If Dad finds out I went, he'll just have to deal with it.

~ Josie, 15

A Family Disease

When I was a child, life was very confusing. On the outside, my family looked like the "perfect, all-American family." Two parents, three kids, nice house. I had everything I could ever ask for, and felt loved. But on the inside, things were very strange. My mother often fell asleep right after dinner. She rarely offered to drive me anywhere, and didn't get involved in any of my activities. Her favorite thing to do was to shop, and she did it often. Shopping was the only thing we did together. My father worked long, hard hours, managing a company in the town where we lived. He probably had to work that hard just to pay my mother's outrageous bills!

I'll never forget the day my father gathered my brothers and I together and told us why Mom had been acting so strange. "Your Mom is an alcoholic," he said. My heart sank. Everything I knew about alcoholism I had learned on television. I pictured drunks lying in the gutter. But as I thought about the events of the last few years, it all became clear. My mom was a "closet drinker." I never saw the bottles. She would even put booze in her mouthwash bottles to hide it from my dad.

This discovery was the beginning of a long, hard road to recovery for us all. Alcohol had put us in a dangerous family trance for years, and the problems didn't automatically end when the drinking stopped. It took a very long time for the denial to wear away and for my family to recognize how we each played a role in my mother's drinking.

Alcoholism, like all addictions, affects not only the one who is addicted, but family members and those they love. I thought I could control my Mom's drinking. I thought if I just said the right thing, or did the right thing, or made her happy, she would stop drinking. Not true. I was as powerless over alcoholism as she was.

When I was twenty-five years old, I finally began to realize how my mom's alcoholism had affected me and my ability to have honest, open relationships. I got help from friends and a therapist. I learned a lot about the disease and how it had tainted my life. I am proud to say that I have gotten out from under the nasty effects of alcoholism, and my mom has, too. Our family is now more honest and open than it has ever been.

If you or someone else you know is growing up in an alcoholic family, don't wait any longer to get help. Find out about Alateen and Al-Anon, or talk to an adult you trust. Learn about the disease and how it captures those who get stuck in its web. You are not alone. Even "perfect, all-American families" sometimes have deep, dark secrets. Get free. Get some help.

~ ANONYMOUS, 38

Troubled kids walk on broken glass that their parents shattered.

We need to give them shoes.

Sarah, 15

Addictions have a way of sneaking up on us, and we're usually unaware of the consequences until it's too late. This teen writes about her chemical dependency ~ the choices she made, and the denial of her problems. She closes by asking you to really look at your life instead of hiding from it.

TRASHED TEST DUMMIES

I chose the life of the street.

I thought I could conquer it on my own two feet.

I chose the life of a driven drunk.

Doing it 'cause I always felt free.

I drank 'til I was drunk, to hide my feelings.

I drank 'til I was trashed, staring at walls and ceilings.

It was fun until the day was done.

But the next day, another drink…

Covering up so I didn't have to think.

Trust me, it's a life many of us choose.

It's a life we own, we just don't know whose.

Where to turn, what to do,

Not ever really having a clue.

Sit back, my friend. Look at your situation.

This is life…it's not a dream or your imagination.

~Sarah, 16

The majority of teens with eating disorders are girls. Some girls will go to dangerous lengths to achieve a particular "look," or to make a statement to the people around them about a variety of issues. Meanwhile, their health reaches a dangerous point. There is no quick treatment for this illness, and the effects are long lasting, as this young woman explains.

My Friend, Food

My eating disorder is what I remember most about my adolescence. It began when I was thirteen. I was healthy again by age fifteen, but the feelings and effects of that time remain with me today.

It all began when we moved to a new town, far away from where I grew up. I was in the middle of junior high school. Food became my friend when I had to leave all my old friends behind. I was extremely lonely, and angry with my parents for making us move.

Eating helped make the pain go away. I began to gain extra weight, and my parents suggested that I go on a diet. It didn't work at first, but eventually, with exercise and counting calories, I lost weight and looked thin like everyone told me I should. People who hadn't paid any attention to me before started to comment on how good I looked. I continued to lose weight so people would keep saying those positive comments. At the time, I really didn't like myself. I didn't have the right clothes, I didn't have a boyfriend, I wasn't good at sports, and I didn't fit in with the "cool kids." My only chance at getting people to like me was to stay thin.

Eventually, I became too thin. My health was in danger, and I was hospitalized. I continued to get a lot of attention, which was what I craved. Focusing so much on my eating disorder also made me look at the conflicting things involved with becoming a teenager. I wanted to grow up and away from my parents, yet I was fearful of separating. I wanted to be the complete opposite of Mom, but I didn't know how to be different. I liked boys, but was afraid to get too close to them physically. I felt out of control of my emotions, which normally happens to teens, but I didn't want to *ever* feel out of control. Eating too much, then getting sick, helped me avoid those things for a long time. And I was still in control.

With time, counseling, and medical care, I started to get well. I finally looked at those teenage issues and allowed myself to feel the feelings. It was scary! But each time I faced a fear and took a risk to try something new, I learned more about myself. I learned that I was a lot stronger than many people believed. I could handle more than I thought I could. One of the most important lessons I learned was that how you feel about yourself is more important than how you look.

Sometimes life is painful, but friends and family can be helpful if you just ask. It can be really hard to grow up…kind of like getting stuck in a maze and not having a clue how to get out. One of the best things you can do is learn to trust yourself, and listen to what your heart is telling you. It's part of you, and it won't take you anywhere you don't have the strength to go.

~ ERIN, 23, COLLEGE STUDENT

A parent's illness or medical problems of your own can suddenly change the patterns, the routines, and the stability of your life. Look for the lessons learned in the following stories. Through pain comes strength….

Seeing Red

The bright red lights on the ambulance circled around and around our front yard, illuminating the trunks of the old maple trees with every turn. It was the middle of the night, and my Dad was being rushed to a medical center forty miles away. He had been bleeding internally throughout the evening, and the situation had gone from bad to worse. My older brother was away at college, and my mother was torn about leaving me behind, all alone in the house, all alone with my emotions. I was fourteen at the time, but I felt quite grown up and suddenly very responsible. I assured Mom that I would be all right, then watched her climb into the back of the ambulance to be with Dad.

I looked out my bedroom window as the ambulance drove across our front yard and away into the darkness. I did not know if my Dad would return. I worried that the driver would go too fast and have an accident on some distant highway. I also worried that he would go too slow and not get to the emergency room on time. The bright red lights were gone, but the scene was already etched in my mind. I'm certain that I didn't fall back to sleep that night.

Dad was in the hospital for over a month. Throughout my teens and well into my adult years, he was hospitalized many times. We lived over an hour away from the hospital, yet every evening when Mom returned home from work and I came home from school, the two of us would drive to the hospital to visit Dad. We ate dinner in the hospital cafeteria, and I did my homework in the car by the light of a flashlight. Our family life had changed for good, but Dad was alive. Mom shouldered many extra burdens, while Dad suffered in his own way, too. It was also a difficult time for me, but I still enjoyed my teenage years.

Many years have passed since those ambulance lights cut through the darkness. Dad survived years of medical care, and is healthy today. I've had to reassure Mom at least a hundred times that it was okay to leave me alone that night. I've also learned that family life can literally change overnight, and that a teenage girl left alone in her room on a frightening night of crisis can learn from it, change directions, and move on.

~ DEB, 40

Mom's Limits, Mom's Strength

Several years ago, my mother became physically disabled. At first her doctor told her that there was nothing wrong, that it was "all in her head." Eventually she was diagnosed with multiple sclerosis. People finally knew that she was not faking her symptoms. It was very real, especially for her and those of us in her family. Mom took it hard at first, but was thankful that she knew what the problem was.

My Mom has become a very strong person emotionally, and is determined to overcome her handicaps. Many people look up to her because of her mental strength, and in spite of being held back by her physical body, she is still able to help many people in need. Mom is often completely exhausted, but never turns away a friend who needs to talk. Just watching her would give anyone strength. Some days she can barely move her legs, but she still gets up and cheerfully greets my brothers and me in the morning.

Living with my mother has taught me many lessons. We take many things for granted when we are healthy. I respect Mom more, seeing how she handles her limits each day. She is a truly special person.

~ Amy, 16

When a young person dies, it all feels wrong and out of order somehow. This person learned an important lesson after her friend died....

Losing a Friend Forever

I moved to a new town in the middle of fifth grade, leaving my best friend behind. We wrote to each other a lot at first, then occasionally, and eventually we lost touch. I still went back to my old house on weekends to visit my mother, but my old friend and I had lost our connection somehow.

One day this summer, my stepmother came into my bedroom and asked if I had known this girl, Leanne. I said yes, and asked if Leanne had called me. My stepmother just shook her head, then told me that Leanne had been hit by a car, and had died the next day. Suddenly, boys, clothes, and cliques weren't important any more. All I could think about was how fragile life was, and how we never know when it might end.

I went to Leanne's funeral, and realized how pathetic it was to have stopped communicating with her. Now I could never be in touch with her. All that remained was a vacant body. Every tear that I shed that day represented one of her many wonderful traits.

Stay in touch with those who are important to you. You just never know....

~ Erika, 13

Young people and adults often have very strong feelings about teen pregnancy. Life for the pregnant teen literally changes overnight. Tough decisions need to be made; relationships with parents and friends change. This writer tells of her feelings about her best friend's situation.

Respect

I am fourteen years old, and my best friend, Michelle, is pregnant. She had sex with some guy, and now she's pregnant. How could she? We were supposed to be friends forever, graduate together, go to college together, Be in each other's weddings, and then have babies. Now it's all messed up.

My Mom called me into her room the other day. She said she wanted to talk about what happened to Michelle. I couldn't look at her. She said, "Boys don't respect girls who have sex with them. Do you understand?" "Yeah, I understand," I said.

I left as soon as I could and went to my room. I tried to understand, but I don't. Does this mean that Dad didn't respect Mom when they had sex and made me? Do girls respect boys they have sex with? Can two people who are not married respect each other if they have sex? And what about love? Is respect more important than love?

I need to talk to somebody about this. It's all very confusing. The only thing I know is that I'm glad I'm not Michelle.

~ TATIANA, 14

The number of rapes reported in the U.S. is increasing. This writer did not know the girl who was attacked in her neighborhood, but she still felt the effects of the crime.

After Dark

A girl was raped on my street last night. She was thirteen years old, just like me. My mother read about it in the newspaper this morning, and as I left for school, she gave me an extra hug and told me to be careful.

Suddenly my neighborhood feels different. I always thought it was safe to walk the four blocks home from school, safe to walk home after dark from my friends' houses or from the neighborhood center where I go a lot. Now I'll have to be looking all around, wondering if there is someone hiding nearby, ready to hurt me like he hurt that girl. I wonder if she always thought our street was safe too, and I wonder what must be going through her head today. I wasn't raped, but I still feel like something was stolen from me, from our neighborhood, from women everywhere last night.

I really don't need this on my mind right now...there are plenty of other things for me to think about. I'm trying to get my grades up, because I'll start high school next year and I want to do well. I'm dealing with changes in my body that feel strange. I want to go out with a boy I like, but Mom says I'm too young for that. One of my friends started smoking last week, and I really want to help her quit. Why do all these things have to happen at the same time?

And why did that guy have to rape that girl and give me more to worry about? She was only thirteen, just like me.

~ CARMEN, 13, MAD AND SAD

Quietly Fighting Back

It is one of those rainy days in New York City. People are huddled inside their raincoats like turtles in their shells. The subway is crowded as I travel to school that morning, but I find a seat way in the back. All the seats are soon taken, and many people are standing up, holding onto the metal rings that hang from the ceiling. I pull out my big, heavy science book to study for an exam. By concentrating really hard on the reading in front of me, I can avoid eye contact with the other passengers.

As I sit there reading my textbook, I am vaguely aware of the normal rattling and shaking of the train. I also notice that something is jiggling in front of me, a little bit above my head. With my head still facing down at the book in my lap, I raise my eyes to see what the jiggling is. What I see is the penis of the man who is holding the metal ring right above me. His large raincoat is shielding his private parts from everyone else's eyes but mine.

At first I am scared, thinking of the threat of it all. What else is he planning to do to me? Will he drag me from the subway train and rape me? My face turns bright red, and I pretend to concentrate all the more on my science book. After two or three stops of the train, I realize that he's not going to do anything else. He is just waiting for my reaction. I decide not to have any outward reaction, but in my mind I am thinking, "All I want to do is take this big, heavy textbook and bam! Slam it closed on his penis!"

After a few more stops, the man gets bored. He draws his raincoat together, and gets off the train. I am laughing so hard inside I can barely contain it. It is then that I realize a great truth: Fighting back starts in your head.

~ Po, 42

Too Much to Handle

By the age of eleven I had been molested by my brother, survived years of life with my alcoholic mother, then had to deal with my father's death. So when I was diagnosed with a "stress-related illness" during my first year in college, I wasn't surprised.

I was such a good actress that I fooled everyone time and again. It looked like I was doing fine on the surface, but I still buried everything deep inside of me. Flashbacks of my childhood were showing up more often, I was angry all the time, and I just wanted to die. It seemed like the only solution. I ended up in the emergency room, though, drinking this charcoal stuff to save my life. I was then placed in the "psycho ward," but I fooled them all again, and was released. To what? My anger, and my pattern of putting everyone else's problems before my own. I just couldn't be everything to everyone any longer.

One day during a support group, I heard a woman talk about her daughter's suicide. Hearing her story helped me realize that absolutely no problem is worth dying over, no matter how big or how small. That one person helped me more than all the weeks of hospitalization and months of medication I had had. I will now take life as it comes. I will voice my anger, and not put others first every time. I need to decide where I want to go in my life, and I'm willing to put some work into it. Life really is a journey, not just a destination, and even if you are hit with way too many tough times as a teen, you can pull through and take charge. You and your life are worth it!

~ KELLIE, 24

When we find ourselves in the middle of a tragic situation, it is often difficult to see anything positive to hold on to. However, lessons we learn in the darkest hours of our lives are sometimes the most important ones. The following story is about a young minister who learns about the circle of life through the death of a friend.

Life, Death, and New Life

Today I felt life inside of me for the first time. A little flutter, a teeny kick. I am pregnant with my first child.

Today I was also carried to a new level of understanding about life. Two people in our church have a son who is my age. His wife is expecting their third child; their baby is due a month before ours. He collapsed this morning on the way to the grocery store. The doctors think it was a cerebral hemorrhage.

He is dying. We gathered in the hospital room and gazed at him…over six feet of strong, beautiful man. We caressed him and held him. His parents remembered the other times when they had to let go of him…the first day of school, graduation, when he moved away from home, his wedding.

We cried. We waited. Mother, father, wife, minister, and unborn babies. We stood there in that holy place between life and death and prayed out loud….

> Oh God who gives us breath of life,
>
> Give us the courage to let go of him.
>
> Help us to always remember to say,
>
> "Into Your hands we offer this breath."

Simply by asking, we were filled with love and peace. We let go, and the young man died.

This experience was the greatest gift I have ever received. Life now seems more real to me. Death seems more real, too. When I get scared and look over my shoulder to see which one is closest, I see Jesus. He smiles and says, "Don't worry. We are all in this together."

You and I are part of the circle of life and love.

~ REBECCA, 30

The Flame in Me

I walked into the temple Friday night, depressed over many things in my life. Everyone was exchanging Sabbath greetings, and I managed to smile politely. As the service began, I sat down and mumbled songs with the rest of the congregation. The day's events replayed in my head.

I had cried in school; that hadn't happened in years. But no one seemed to notice or care that I was upset. One friend was willing to listen, but I didn't want to dump all my problems on him. So I didn't say anything this time, and just let him hug me. He told me a few jokes in an attempt to cheer me up. The service seemed to go on forever as I thought about all these things.

Saturday morning, when I came back to Temple, I felt guilty about my lack of concentration the night before. Sad at school; guilty at Temple; changes happening everywhere I turned. I decided to really focus on the melodies of the songs being sung, and even the familiar chanting took on a life of its own. I began to sway with the music, and when I opened my eyes, I saw that many others around the temple were swaying, too. I wasn't as depressed when I left for home.

I had to return with my Dad later that night. As I walked into the dark sanctuary, nothing could be seen except the small, constant light above the Torah. An eternal flame. As I stared up at the flame, I could feel it burning in me. I was going to be all right.

~ ELLIE, 16

The Men in Our Lives

Messages from Dads and Men Who Father

Most of what we know about being women, we learn from the females in our lives. But each of us has both feminine and masculine energy within us. It is important to remember that the men in our world have wisdom that can support and empower women as well.

Daddy. Dad. Poppa. Think about your father for just a moment. Bring a picture of him into your mind, and notice how you feel. For many of us, thinking about our relationships with our dads stirs us up. Reflecting on the emotional bond between fathers and daughters may leave us feeling a sense of longing for a relationship we don't have, or a tender thankfulness for the love we feel with our dads. Our fathers are the very first male role models we have. By observing them and the other significant men in our lives, we learn about maleness and how women and men relate, and we begin to recognize and develop our own masculine energy.

These messages from dads reflect the love and mutual respect that can exist between fathers and daughters. If you don't have a dad or a father figure in your life, look for an adult male mentor. Open your heart to the kind of deep connection that fathers and daughters can share.

Lessons in the Fog

We set out late to drive you to your girlfriend's birthday party, and didn't give much thought to the foot of snow on the ground from last week's storm. The weather was warmer now, mostly wet and foggy. We both had a rough idea of how to get to your friend's house: it was set back from the road, on a hill, on the left, somewhere after you had driven for a long time.

It was too dark for you to see me smiling at the fog and at our slow pace. This would give us some time to talk, something I worried might become rare as you began your fourteenth year. We crept through the fog, watching for house lights, deer in the road, and for ruts that hadn't been plowed this far away from town. We continued uphill with a bit of confidence, but mostly were afraid to slow down and lose our momentum. Finally, we were both convinced that we were lost. We stopped driving.

How was it that we made all the right turns, but now found ourselves in the midst of this foggy nowhere? We rolled down the windows to try to get our bearings. Outside it was beautiful, almost magical, like a scene in a storybook forest. But we were sitting in a muddy mistake! Now our simple evening errand was turning into an adventure. We laughed, in spite of nearly getting stuck, got the car turned around, and headed back to correct our mistake. Eventually we found the right house. You joined your friends at the party, and I left for home with time to think.

I love that we're alike in so many ways…we are both talkers, and we share similar temperaments. We even sense how the other is thinking sometimes. Watching you through the last fourteen years has given me a chance to grow up again, and to see it this time through the eyes of a girl. The issues seem to be mostly the same…feeling uncertain and confused, with many chances for mistakes.

I've watched you ease your way out of childhood, but I still find myself trying to protect the little girl you used to be. And I care a lot more about what you think of me. I realize that we're heading for the days when as adults we will be equals, but for now, if I can be your hero sometimes, that's great! When we put our heads together, like tonight in the fog, we can make mistakes, yet end up in the right place after all. I know

I'm glad for our adventure. It gave us both a chance to learn from each other, laugh, turn ourselves around, and get on with the party.

~ ANONYMOUS, 46

My Daughters, My Friends

My daughters are wonderful! They are smart, funny, energetic, and have a keen social awareness. They are also stubborn, individualistic, and often seem to be from another planet, not just another generation! But I do feel that our family continues to grow in affection and knowledge the longer we know one another.

When I look back over the years, I wonder…what part did I really play in my daughters' lives? I thought I knew what to do and what not to do. Don't be too sparing or too generous, too strict or too indulgent, don't expect over-achievement, but don't let them be lazy. I promised myself I would not be an "absentee father." But real life was not what I had expected, and I slipped into the pattern of letting my wife do it all. I found it easy to escape into my busy work life. I made fun of my daughters' favorite music, urged them to get better grades at school, and forgot about letting them seek their own interests. Then something changed. When I found that it was useless to make fun of The Beatles and push my daughters to like classical music, I started listening to their music with them. I stopped being such an authority figure in their lives when I found that my daughters were actually asking reasonable questions and weren't just out to break my rules. I began to enjoy being with them, and started to be a "student" rather than a "teacher" in many ways. None of this changed rapidly, and there are still issues that divide us. My youngest likes to watch David Letterman each night, and I can't stand that show, but I feel it is a tribute to us both if this is the worst thing I can say!

My daughters and I are friends now. We're not just family. We walk and jog together, we help each other around our homes and yards, and love to discuss books and movies. We are a blessed group of people who enjoy being with each other more than we enjoy our friends. Who could ask for anything more?

~ JUD, 67, GENERAL INTERNIST

My Daughters Drive the Cars!

I'm the father of triplet, preteen daughters. When our three daughters were born, most people said, "Great!" or "How nice!," but I could see in their eyes a degree of pity because I didn't have at least one son. There is still a strong belief in our society that your family is somehow incomplete until you have a son. I wouldn't trade a daughter for half a dozen sons, and I sure wouldn't think of trading six daughters for one son! I've seen sons. I was a son. I know what we can be like.

But still, I'm worried for my daughters. To be a female in American society today is to be "genderly challenged," in the same way that one who is blind is considered "visually challenged." Maybe it's more accurate to say that females are "sexually challenged." Lord knows that most females have to fight off the sexual challenges of testosterone-driven men. I'm more worried, though, about the strong message that is beaten daily into the minds of men and women and boys and girls. This message is that boys are best and girls are dependent. There are countless books where young men rescue helpless maidens, movies where male actors get the mega-millions and actresses get half as much, television commercials where the men drive the cars and the women do the laundry. I refuse to raise laundresses! My daughters will drive the cars!

My girls are going to be presidents or senators or business tycoons, not because that would mean they were truly successful in life, but because they would all be good presidents, senators, or business tycoons! They might be poets or scholars or artists. And I hope they spend some time being moms too, because being a parent means fun and snuggles and good times. Mostly I hope that I'm raising happy, secure, loving humans who will survive the craziness of American society today, and having survived it, will in turn raise daughters, or maybe even sons, who will truly see the wonder and worth of having and being daughters.

~ JOHN, 43

Remembering

Dearest Daughter,

If I made any positive contributions to your incredible journey to womanhood, I can tell you that they were more from good fortune than from wisdom. I probably started out on the wrong foot because my rusty old generation wanted me to believe that it was easier for a father to relate to a son than to a daughter. When your older brother came along, fatherhood was all that I had expected it to be. I could relate to this little male. Then you entered the world. The idea of sharing my life with this small female person was challenging, to say the least! But it was still exciting, and I learned faster than you did at that point in our lives.

Thank God I realized, when you were still very young, that I had no reason to expect any less from you, just because some of your body parts were different from your brother's! I think we followed our hearts through those early years, while we struggled to be a family and to make the goodness of God a part of our lives. You and I learned to communicate in ways that even now, I don't fully understand.

Then along came this thing called "adolescence." Before my very eyes, you were becoming a woman. I knew nothing about rites of passage or the female version of "the birds and the bees." I continued to see my role as one of encouragement and support. Through adolescence and boyfriends and college, through your career and marriage and children of your own, there has never been a day when I have felt disconnected from your life or unimportant to you.

When I faced a very difficult time in my own life, I realized how much my strength and wisdom comes from my children. I only hope that by supporting you and being respectful of your individuality, I have been a source of strength for you, too.

~ Love, Dad

Can't Go Back

Being a father didn't come naturally to me… I had to learn it from my kids. I don't know how they graded me then, or how they'd rate me now that they're grown and have kids of their own. But I know there is a difference between simply being a father and being a good one. When it all began, however, I didn't have a clue about what I was doing.

In the fifties and sixties, it was not fashionable for men to do the laundry, change diapers, feed a baby…all those things that I felt I could and should do. Men were never taught how to talk to children, tickle them, or play with them on the floor. They didn't know when to let them win at checkers, how to comfort them when they were hurting, or what advice to give them as they grew. I learned how to be a parent through experience; it was simply trial and error.

I really wanted to be a good father, but my alcoholism and my children's adolescence were a lethal combination. I'm sure I said and did things then that I wouldn't dream of doing now. But I can't go back and be a different father, just as my children can't go back and relive their teenage years. I regret my outbursts of anger, my unreasonable rules, not listening to my children closely, the mistakes I didn't admit to, and using marijuana in front of them. But I did the best that I could at the time, even though my children remind me that it still wasn't enough. I believe I was a better parent to my children than my parents were to me, and my children can build on that as they help their own daughters and sons along this journey called life.

~ DONALD, 67, COLLEGE PROFESSOR

"But Mommy, When Does Daddy Cry?"

Last night I was looking through photo albums, thinking about my life. One of the pictures reminded me of a day when you were very young and your mom was crying. You asked, "Mommy, when does Daddy cry?" I don't remember how your mom responded at the time, but now I know the answer.

I don't cry often, but my tears flow at times of great joy and of deep sorrow. I'll never forget the day your mom and I were married. I stood at the altar, watching her move effortlessly down the aisle. For the first time as an adult, uncontrollable tears of gratitude and joy welled up inside me.

A few years later, when you were born, I held you closely in my arms. I wept, amazed by how much I loved you. On Christmas Eve, when you were just two months old, you played the baby Jesus. Your mom and I were Mary and Joseph. I remember looking down at you lying in the manger, and I cried tears of joy. When you had spinal meningitis as a child, I cried because I couldn't imagine life without you. Sometimes I would sneak into your room at night, stand by your bed, and watch you sleep. My love for you was so deep that it overflowed in wet salty droplets that would land on your fuzzy blankets.

Now, you are a teenager, and I become teary-eyed with pride at your swim meets. When I listen to you singing in the choir or when I read one of your poems, I am moved beyond words. Every time I go to a wedding, I cry. I remember the joy of my own wedding and my love for your mom, but I also imagine a day when it may be you walking down the aisle. Letting go will be hard. Maybe I am just practicing.

I cried many tears at my grandmother's funeral, surprised at how difficult it was to say goodbye to her. She and I were not very close in the last part of her life. But as I sat and listened to people talking about her, I realized just how important she had been to me. She loved me no matter what, and embraced the very parts of me that have been the secret to my success as an adult.

When does Daddy cry? Dad cries at events centered on the women in his life; the women he loves, and who are responsible for him being here. He is most deeply touched by the women who have changed his life, and the girls who bring him great pride and joy. These are the women of your heritage. One of these women is you! Thank you for giving me reasons to cry. Tears remind me of what is important.

~ DAVE, 39, FATHER OF
TWO GREAT YOUNG WOMEN

Dad's Big Test

"Dad, what would you do if I got pregnant in high school?" You asked me this while you were washing the dishes one evening. Suddenly, all these worries rushed through my mind. Is she pregnant? Is she serious? Is she just trying to tell me how mature she is now? I caught my breath. This question is a big test for a dad, you know!

What should a dad say to questions like this? I love you more than anything, sweetheart. I was there when you were born. I watched the nurse take you immediately into the next room to help you breathe better and live. I held you proudly and hugged you numerous times, whenever Mom wasn't hugging you!

I watched you take your first step on your own. You were proudly wearing your new blue dress, made by your grandmother. As you took those big, wide steps with your arms stretched out for balance, I cheered you on and hugged you mightily when you made it. Remember when we would go see The Nutcracker ballet each Christmas? It was always just you and I. You loved to dance so much. And when we got you your own piano, you began to play so beautifully. I was always such a musical klutz, and was so happy that you could master something that I could not.

I remember when you graduated from eighth grade, standing proud and tall, growing into a lovely young woman. So when you ask me what I would do if you got pregnant, I know this is a big step, like those first steps taken when you were a little girl. I know that you want the love of a young man your age, and I know that you deserve to become a loving mother to your own baby someday. I know you have friends who have been pregnant. What am I supposed to say?

Well, I managed to stammer, "Mom and I will always love you, and will take care of you as long as you need us to. But I hope you'll get married first, before you have a baby." I hope it was the right thing to say. It came from my heart.

You stood there at the sink, overflowing with dishes, thinking it through. You then replied, "I think I will wait to have a baby until I get married." I smiled and inwardly thanked God. Then I knew. I knew that you were no longer a girl. That day, you were a woman.

~ LEE, 53

First Blood

At her first period I wanted to give my daughter a special gift. My wife bought roses and a topiary plant. I thought of earrings, pearls, a jewelry box, but nothing seemed right. Then I found the perfect present~a gold watch from Switzerland: behind the hands, dark blue sky, stars, and the changing phases of the moon.

That night at dinner she wanted to play down the change. She doesn't like moments to become too "ritually." With each gift she asked, "Why are you giving me this?" When I gave her the watch, she simply said, "Thank you." A few days later, they started bombing Iraq. She set her new watch to Baghdad time.

~ ALTON, 57, TEACHER, COUNSELOR, DANCER, CATCHER IN THE RYE

A Note on Boys

Let me tell you something about boys. There is a magical moment in an adolescent boy's life when he suddenly realizes that girls are more than people to be teased. This moment brings with it a transformation in a boy's soul, because suddenly he decides to "care." He cares about how he looks, how he smells, how he talks, how he eats, who he sits with, and who is watching him play the sport he used to love more than anything else in the whole wide world. Now all he seems to be able to do is fall flat on his face while she's over there, ignoring him. He cares about someone he's afraid to ask to the dance, because then he'd have to call her on the phone and then his friends would make fun of him because they could say he "loved her" if he actually did ask her to the dance. Unfortunately, just when he needs to become sophisticated, this is the moment he becomes really goofy. Without a clue as to what is happening to him, he is from this moment on going to be defining himself not by what the guys think of him, but by what the girls think of him. His life has changed forever, and the poor guy doesn't even know why. That moment came for me one morning when a female classmate of mine walked up to my never-before-voluntarily-combed hair, tousled it, and said, "You'd be really cute if you combed your hair once in a while."

Now, I'd known some girls who were okay to talk to, or even to sit with at lunch, but it was if I'd been struck by lightning! I can still remember the time of day, the exact place in the hallway at school, and even what she was wearing when she spoke those words to me more than thirty years ago. I couldn't wait to run home and get in the shower so I could wash and comb my hair. I have never been the same since!

Which gets me to the point of this message. Girls are powerful! You have the power to change a young boy from a loud, boring, smelly old sneaker into a timid, tongue-tied, clean young shoe. Like any explosive energy, this is a power that you should not use carelessly. Adolescence is a time of terrible questioning for boys. They are leaving their safe, male world of bikes and skateboards and rude noises, and entering into your unknown teenage world of parties and dancing and polite conversations. Boys are not prepared for it, and will probably spend the rest of their adult lives trying to figure out how it happened.

So here's what I'm asking from you as the holder of this secret energy. Try to reach deep inside yourselves and find strength~a strength that will allow you to control this power that can magically transform boys at the exact moment that they are the most vulnerable to this change. Be gentle, and understand that a few choice words from you in the hallway outside the cafeteria can shape the very future of a boy's life.

My "eighth grade vision" moved away in the tenth grade. I might have been cute when I combed my hair, but I was still the shortest guy in the class, and after stopping me in the hall that morning, she never gave me another thought! But when you decide to use your power, keep an eye on those cute, short guys. Sometimes they turn out to be the ones who will actually listen to what you have to say!

~ CHRISTOPHER, 44

Phone Calls

You have begun to receive phone calls from...a boy! This is new, it's exciting, it's scary, but it's okay. These feelings that you have talked about are just what I'm going through, too. You seem happy with his calls; you go to your room and chat for awhile, then hang up, and he often calls back again. I remember asking you if his parents knew about his phone calls. You said you weren't sure. I have asked you if you like him, if you think he respects you, if he is nice to you, if he is honest with you. I think that one of the important qualities of a good friendship or romance is that you are not afraid to let others know about it.

I know that this is a new experience for you, and you seem to be enjoying the extra attention it brings, both from family and friends. As your father, I have watched you change so much. I was there when you were born, held you when you cried, changed endless diapers, hugged you when you fell down, asked you repeatedly to set the table, to turn out the lights in your room, checked on your homework, and now you are moving on to something new. Boys!

It is so important to remember that you have the right to think and feel whatever you want. Do not let anyone make you say or do something that does not feel right in your heart. I know that as you grow up, boys and others will become even more important in your life, and you may not want to share everything with me or with Mom. We were teenagers once, too, even if that is hard to believe! And we still remember what it was like to be thirteen and in love and totally confused. I believe that as your father, I can offer my guidance, my love, my reassurance, maybe even some answers. And as hard as it is sometimes, I can also give you space.

Remember that I am always here for you, and that I love you very much.

~ Russ, 39

Is Anybody Listening?

A good friend of mine was driving to the store with his eight-year-old daughter last week when a huge thunderstorm hit. Lightning flashed. Thunder roared, and the rain was so heavy that he could barely see the road. Like usual, his daughter talked nonstop. She told her dad about her day and asked question after question. My friend listened carefully and answered her questions, but his eyes were glued to the road. He was intent on getting them safely to the store and back home again.

Finally, frustrated that her dad wouldn't look at her, the daughter said in exasperation, "Daddy, are you listening to me? Why don't you look at me when I am talking to you?" My friend replied, "Just because I am not looking at you doesn't mean that I don't hear you. I still care about you, I just have to watch the road now."

My friend went on to explain that God communicates with us in much the same way. We cannot see or touch or e-mail God, but a divine spirit is listening to us always. Faith is our relationship with God.

A parent's love can be much the same. Unconditional love is based on a faith that we can be loved for who we are…even with zits, gross boyfriends, weird music, and all of our faults. So if you ever question whether your parents love you, think of the little girl in the thunderstorm. Her dad could not look at her or touch her, but they could still communicate their love through faith.

~ ROGER, FATHER OF FOUR DAUGHTERS

LETTING GO

Your time to be a little girl won't come again.

That thought may be sad to someone who doesn't know

How beautiful your youth has been.

The memories of loving and learning will live forever.

But now...

Your future as a woman is even more exciting.

You are a masterpiece.

You go now, to bring beauty to the world,

To be a strong woman of great compassion.

As you step away, Rejoice!

For whatever distance comes between us,

I will share your days of sunshine, and help whisk away the

clouds,

Our hearts bound together,

In a special love.

~Sterling, 47

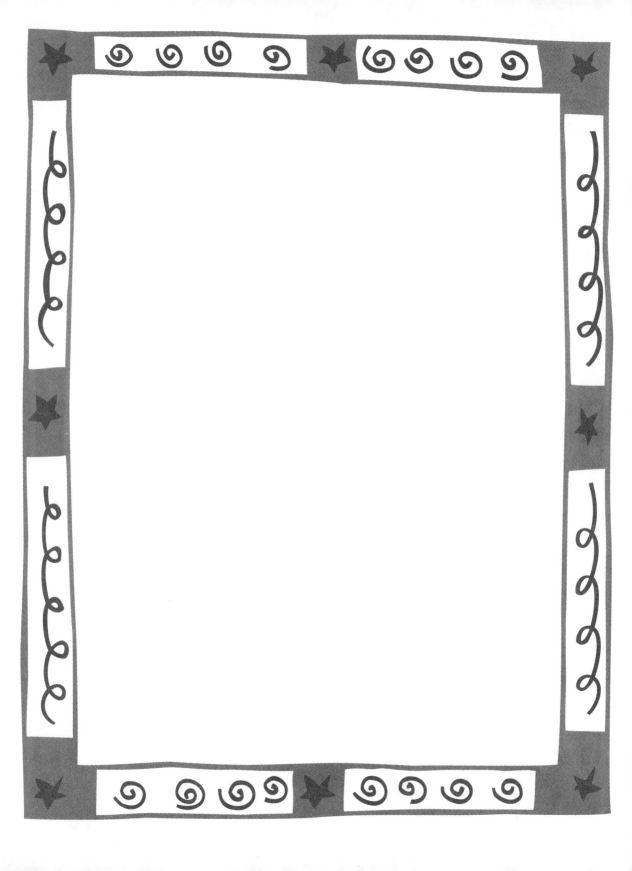

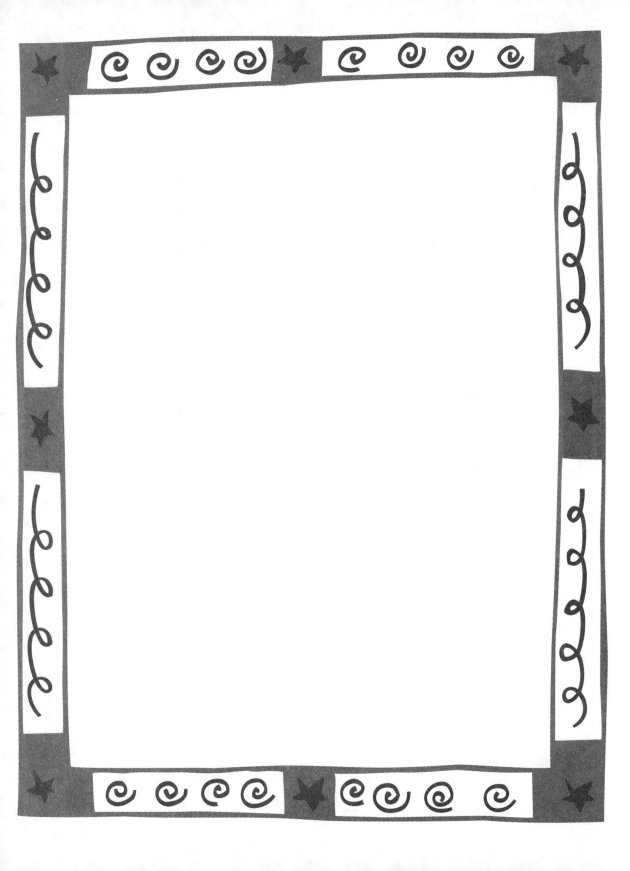

Honoring This Time

Treasures, Blessings, and Dreams 10

he transitions that you are going through can be difficult at times, but you will make it! You will be stronger, wiser, and feel a deeper sense of connection to women and girls everywhere as you begin your journey to discover the mysteries of being female.

The pages ahead are full of positive messages for you as you walk along the path to womanhood. Read them when you need a loving reminder that "it will be all right," or when you just need reassurance that other women have experienced what you are dealing with today. This is a time to be honored, not hurried along. Many women have shared a part of themselves so that you can feel strong and ready as you move away from your girlhood days and take your first steps toward the woman you are becoming. We are in this together, and even if you are feeling alone, remember that girls and women everywhere are sending blessings and good thoughts your way!

A Time to Ask

Being an adolescent is like living in a box of surprises. You never know what is coming along next! It is a time to test the waters; a time to begin to stand on the foundation of all that you have learned through the years. It is a time to remember to honor your parents, even when you may not understand them. Adult emotions are surging into young bodies, and you might be thinking about where you have come from and where you are going. It is a time to think about what your friends are into, and whether you want to be into those things, too. It is also a time to ask your parents to trust your judgment when it comes to friends, clothes, and music.

Mainly, it is a time to ask questions...hard questions. Talk to adults and ask about choices they have made and how those choices affected them over the years. The right choices are sometimes difficult to make, but when you get older and look back on these years, you will probably discover that the results of those tough decisions ended up being the most rewarding.

This can be a time of great joy! Look for the hidden treasures inside yourself. You are in the middle of a very special season of your life. You will never be able to pass through it again, but someday you can pass on all that you learn to someone else living in a box of surprises.

~ MICHELLE, 37, MOTHER

Cocoons and Butterflies

You can be a butterfly, young woman. You have been in your cocoon too long. You are ready. Although the struggle isn't over, you have come so close, so close to breaking the outer shell that holds you back.

Now is comfortable. What lies ahead is frightening. Come close and let go of your inhibitions. You can embrace your dreams and then you will glide. Majestic, young woman, you will glide to where your Earth mother calls you. You will find yourself shimmering by the moon's glow. You will hold your head up high, and gracefully arch your way, as you stand and look out upon it all.

~ AIDE, 20

The Garden Path

As you step into your teenage years, remember that you are still on the same path that you started on at your birth. You will continue along this path your whole life, always changing and always growing, no matter what your age.

If you think of yourself as a flower garden and life as the world around you, there will always be something bursting up and blossoming, while something else is withering away at the same time. It happens with gardens…and it happens with people, too. This depends on what season of life you are in, and how the weather is all around you. It might be spring; it might be sunny and warm. There might be a snowstorm or a mudslide, or maybe it feels like there is a hurricane on the way, just ready to swirl you out into the dark night. But you are the same garden you've always been, and you can handle any changes that occur. When something is painful and makes you sad, it is because a beautiful, new flower is rising up from deep within you. You will learn the most from these difficult times, even though it might be scary, too.

As a gardener takes care of her flowers and plants, remember to take care of yourself. There is nothing more important than nurturing your body, your mind, and your spirit. In order to succeed, try to accept the changes that occur as a natural way of learning what you need to know. Look at changes as challenges, and you will learn to welcome them. Changes will be the newest flowers in your garden, and it will be more beautiful than ever!

~ KATRINA, 37

Honor Roll

Excitement, change, challenge, fear. What a time this is for you! Take some time to honor this period of transition. Sit quietly with yourself now and then, and think of those people who inspire you. Make a list of these people, and write down what you honor in them. Next, think about yourself. What are some things about you that you respect and honor? Make a list…only *you* have to ever see it. It's your "honor roll" of self-appreciation and respect. Support the challenge of this journey into independence by placing yourself and others on your private honor roll.

~ CHERYL, 46,
MOM AND PSYCHOTHERAPIST

Changing Dreams

Don't forget to dream! And in your dreams, don't be limited by the possible. Dream of the outrageous, dream of the impossible! As young girls, our dreams are boundless. We dream of being a star or a moon as easily as we dream of being a bug or a mouse. We charge through the universe, always seeing it through the eyes of the creatures we encounter.

As we grow up, our focus narrows to the human realm. We look at only what humans can see, dream only about what humans can do. We limit ourselves to what each of us thinks she can actually do. We limit ourselves to the professions and accomplishments that we see as within reach. Slowly, oh so slowly, we lose the ability to dream. Later, when we are asked what we want to be or what we want to do, we are empty, and can only tell what we are.

Don't forget to dream!

~ ROBIN, MOTHER OF
THREE YOUNG WOMEN

Late one afternoon, in a circle of girls and women of many generations, these good wishes and words of encouragement were exchanged. Let yourself be lifted by these words from one heart to another....

The sky is the limit. Believe it!

You are the captain of your own ship. The decisions you make affect your future and the path your ship takes through life.

Listen with your heart and not just with your ears.

Smile and be yourself.

You are the artist of your life. Paint freely, allow yourself to be creative, and have fun.

Be confident and happy with yourself. There is only one you in the entire world!

Being a girl is great!

Remember that all the wisdom you need is in your heart right now.

You are very strong, even if you don't realize it yet.

Your beauty comes from within. Let it shine on those around you.

We are all sisters born from the same mother, who loves each of us dearly.

Time heals wounds. Stay hopeful about the years ahead, even if life hurts right now.

The Future Is You!

You were born to live in and help form the world of tomorrow. You have a contribution to make to the future of our world. Discovering your own destiny in life requires that you come to know yourself in a new way. Connect with your intuition, know your body and what it tells you, and trust your inner voice to guide you through life.

You are on a journey of self-discovery. To truly find yourself, you will continue to learn all kinds of new skills. When you look outside yourself to find answers to those big questions, you might feel let down or misunderstood. You are the only one who can answer those big questions in your life. Pay attention to your dreams. Speak out when you need to. Go to the wisdom of your own heart to tell you what to do.

~ BETH, 42

All I Want to Say Is...

Listen to others. They may have something important to say.
Learn to love yourself. There may be times when no one else will.
Never give up! You'll be surprised at what you can accomplish.
Live one day at a time. Tomorrow you can start over if you need to.
Consider your possibilities. They are endless!
Don't be afraid. Fear can delay your progress.
Don't just follow the crowd. You may not know where they're going.
Be assertive. You have the wisdom you need right inside of you.
Don't worry about the small stuff. Save your energy for
    the important things.
Share your ideas. They may be worth something someday.

~ SHERYL, 24, ASPIRING SCREENWRITER

"Live your life being the best person you can possibly be." These words are simple, but can help so much as you enter womanhood, friendships, marriage, motherhood, any new phase in life. Things seem to go smoother when you can remember these words and try to live by them.

~ LESLIE, 39

Sounds of the Heart

Adolescence is a time to reflect, to choose, and to decide on many things. Choose wisely what to leave in your past and what to keep as part of you forever. There are some parts of childhood that you simply don't need to leave behind. Take with you the wonder of nature. Rejoice when you see the geese fly south for the winter, or when the first robin shows up in the spring. Slow down and watch a jet streak through the sky, and see the beauty in a single flower.

It is important to always listen to your heart. Today's world is a busy world, but you can choose to take time to be quiet, to still your mind, to dream. Make time to find yourself, for there will never be another you! Believe with all your heart that you are the very best that you could ever be. Now is the time when you can become the person you hold in your dreams.

~ NANCY, 57, DAUGHTER, MOTHER, GRANDMOTHER

Grown-up Woman

It is not always easy becoming a truly grown-up woman. Here are some things about me that help me see the woman I have become.

I accept, respect and love others and myself. I appreciate the stars, the plants, the animals, and other gifts of the natural world. I have a spirituality that sustains me and beautifies my daily life. But when I was younger, what I needed most was a community of women to help me understand what was happening to my mind and to my body as I became the "grown-up woman" I am now. I might have really listened if someone had had an honest conversation with me once in awhile about these things. Find a woman and ask questions. I listen to young women when they talk, and I know you can find someone who will hear you, too.

~ LUISAH, 50

Rooftop Ramblings

When I sit on the porch roof outside my bedroom window, I think about everything! I watch the big night sky, and wonder about the jets that fly overhead, where they are coming from and where they have been. I see the lights of the trucks and cars over on the main highway, and wish I knew where I was going, like they do. The rest of my family is asleep inside the house, but here I sit on the roof. I'm always thinking of so many different things, amazed that anyone can ever sleep when there is so much to figure out about life and the future and where I'll be in ten years.

There is something out there bigger than me. It feels like God, and it feels like me plus all the people I know, and all the places I've been to. It's something really huge that I'm just beginning to see and be a part of.

I like this feeling! And even though some might think I have a simple little life, far away from big cities or anything exciting, I'm on the verge of something great. I'm a part of the big picture. I can go where those jets are going. My life matters.

~ LEXIE, 15

CROSSROADS

You stand at the crossroads, bare feet on solid ground.

You're becoming a woman.

Let your guide be the sounds

Of the voices of women and girls in your life,

Of the voice deep within you, courageous and wise.

We are in this together, but your life is your own.

In this circle of women, you're never alone.

In celebration,

Deb

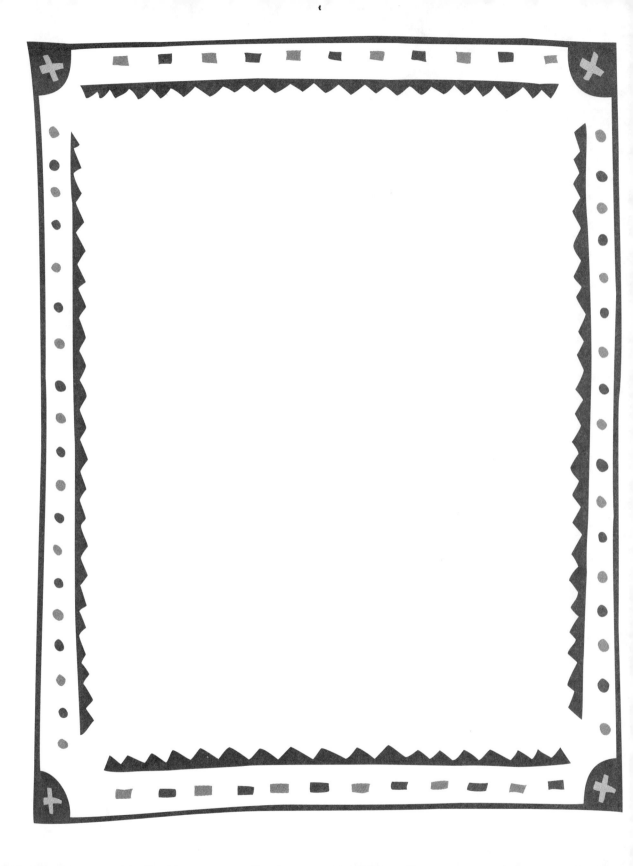

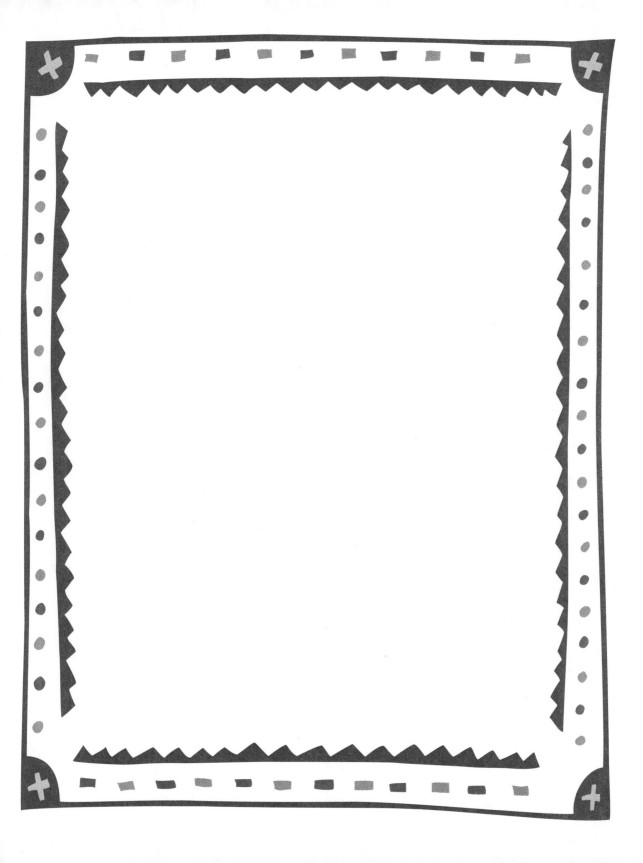

This book is just the beginning! We are currently planning a variety of workshops and retreats around the country to celebrate girls and women, and we would love to hear your ideas. If you have a story, poem, or other writings to be considered for inclusion in future publications, please send them our way. We look forward to hearing your thoughts and comments on what you have just read, too. Remember...we're in this together!

For further information, or to submit writings or comments, please contact:

Deb and Bunny
P.O. Box 74
Ithaca, New York 14851

Celestial Arts
P.O. Box 7123
Berkeley, California 94707
website: www.tenspeed.com
orders: order@tenspeed.com

Distributed in Canada by Ten Speed Canada, in the United Kingdom and Europe by Airlift Books, in New Zealand by Tandem Press, in Australia by Simon & Schuster Australia, in Singapore and Malaysia by Berkeley Books, and in South Africa by Real Books.

Cover and interior design by Toni Tajima
Cover collage created by Heather Garnos
Photographs in collage: girls on car by Amanda Brady; girl in hat by Bunny McCune; old family photo from the collection of Pam Cuesta; authors and daughters by Dede Hatch; beach photo courtesy of Heather Garnos.
Author photo on back flap by Dede Hatch
Interior photographs by Dede Hatch, except: page 1 top, 44, 160 top, 200 bottom by Amanda Brady; page 68 bottom, 130 top by Bunny McCune.

Library of Congress Cataloging-in-Publication Data

McCune, Bunny.
    Girls to women, women to girls / Bunny McCune & Deb Traunstein.
       p.   cm
    Summary: Writings by girls and women of all ages explore various aspects of being female: body image and self-esteem, friendships, mother-daughter relationships, sexuality, coping with crises, and more.
    ISBN 0-89087-881-1 (paper)
    1. Women—Psychology—Juvenile literature. 2. Girls—Psychology—Juvenile literature. 3. Women—Biograghpy—Juvenile literature. 4. Girls—Biography—Juvenile literature. [1. Women. 2. Girls. 3. conduct of life.] I. Traunstein, Deb. II. Title.
HQ1206.M263 199
305.42—dc21
                                       98-35798
                                            CIP
                                             AC

First printing, 1998
Printed in the United States

3 4 5 6 7—02 01 00 99

Girls to Women, Women to Girls

Bunny McCune, C.S.W. & Deb Traunstein, C.S.W.

CELESTIAL ARTS
Berkeley, California